CASE INTERVIEW
SUCCESS

Written by TOM ROCHTUS

Printed by
CreateSpace, an Amazon.com Company
Charleston, South Carolina

Table of Contents

Introduction

If you are thinking about a career in consulting, whether management, operational, or another area, this book is for you. Throughout the following chapters, you will find practical advice, tips, and concrete examples that will greatly improve your chances of success and will help you pass interviews with ease and confidence, bringing you closer to the career you are dreaming of!

One major difference between "traditional" interviews and interviews for consulting companies, investment banks, or renowned multinational corporations, is that for the latter the interview process is generally far more complex and takes much more preparation. The focus of this book will principally be on consulting interviews. One well-known example here is, for instance, the "business case", which involves a simulation of a business situation where you need to show your problem-solving capabilities.

Given this, it is crucial that you take your time preparing for the entire application process. First, make sure your resume and cover letter are at their best before sending them to the companies you are interested in. Once invited to interview, you need to allow several days of preparation for each interview, especially during the initial stages of the application process. Keep in mind that you have studied extensively over several years, mainly to get a chance to start an interesting career. Therefore, make a good amount of time free to prepare, and take the interview process very seriously.

About this Book

Before authoring this book, I successfully applied for about all leading management consulting positions. While preparing for the case interviews, I made several pages of notes that I felt could be helpful, and went through these notes before each interview. After going through several applications successfully, I realized that I had built a collection of notes containing valuable information, based on research, experience, and advice from various experts in the field.

I eventually decided to aggregate all the information into a book by bundling the concepts and frameworks that will provide the reader of this book with the necessary skills to succeed consulting interviews. This eventually became the book you are holding right now. Always keep in mind that case interview success is not about luck; it is about being prepared for every possible situation and every possible question.

Why this Book

As you probably know, other books have been written on the topic of preparing for consulting interviews; however, this book differs from those in several aspects. Some of the most important differences this book has, compared to the other books on the topic of consulting interview preparation, are listed below.

First, the most important difference between this book and the other books is that, here, the entire interview process is covered. It has to be said that the business case is just one part of the interview, and to move up to the next round, you will need to succeed along several other dimensions. It is for this reason that the scope of the book also covers the behavioral and psychological aspects of being on a case interview, and gives you a guide from the moment you walk in until the moment you walk out the office doors. This bigger focus, however, does not diminish the importance and relevance of this guide on how to solve business cases.

A second difference is that this book refers to other qualitative sources that supplement the material in this book. My objective is essentially to make you succeed your case interviews, and not to compete with other authors. Therefore I scanned several other sources, and listed the most interesting ones at the end of this book.

Last, to my surprise, several authors of comparable books were never hired by a leading consulting firm. This book is based upon actual successes during the case interview preparations, and the ideas and concepts presented represent positive experiences I have acquired through passing the interview rounds at various top consulting companies.

Chapter I

Your Next Career Move

Before getting into the preparation of your case interview, let us first take a look at the merits and drawbacks of a career in consulting and discuss the different types of business consulting from which you can choose.

It is important to keep in mind that a consulting career is just one of many desirable career options. Without a doubt, when you are at the undergraduate level, you might be considering two or three different career paths. The most common alternatives one considers to a consulting career generally are a corporate career at a global organization or a banking career. Some undergraduates also decide to immediately set out for graduate school, and some even decide to launch their own business.

This chapter not only discusses consulting careers but also briefly covers other career options. It is, however, recommended that you personally investigate each possible career track in greater depth.

CONSULTING CAREERS

Do you get excited about the idea of moving from one location to another or about meeting with top executives? Well, most of the applicants for consulting positions love this idea. Furthermore, the consulting profession is one of the best-paying jobs for recent graduates, offering a very lucrative benefit package while working on some of the most important business issues in various industries. Additionally, there are the many nights in nice hotels, high wage increases, the yearly bonus, and long vacations. This all indeed sounds great, and it is.

It is, however, also important to consider the drawbacks of all this. Very often you will be working in remote locations for four days a week, spending only little time in your hotel and a lot of time with your client.

Keep furthermore in mind that it can be a high-pressure job, and there is a greater risk of being laid off during an economical downturn. Also, most weeks, you would be working about 60 to 75 hours per week; some weeks on the other hand you could be working up to 90 hours per week. If you would then calculate your hourly wage, it might be lower than you expected.

When deciding to apply for a career in consulting, make sure you have understood and considered all the merits and drawbacks related to this type of work. If you feel the advantages of a consulting job significantly outweigh the disadvantages, then becoming a consultant might indeed be something for you. However, always be honest with yourself; if these drawbacks send chills down your spine, then maybe you should consider another career. In the end, the point is not about getting that consulting job, but knowing what you are getting into and truly wanting to become a consultant.

Being motivated and assured of the fact that you would like to be a consultant of course does not guarantee you a job in one of the leading consulting companies. You might have built an impressive resume, but you will still need to prepare for your interview rounds with strong motivation. Always keep in mind that the number of positions available each year is limited and that the number of applicants is enormous. The Boston Consulting Group (BCG), for instance, increased its worldwide consultant headcount by merely 2 percent up to 4,400 in 2009. Similar hiring percentages were found for McKinsey & Company and Bain & Company in that year. Generally, leading consulting firms eventually hire only about 1-4 percent of the applicants. This percentage, of course, strongly depends on the economy and therefore varies from year to year. Take into account that most of these applicants have impressive resumes, and you will understand how difficult it can be to land your dream consulting job.

On the other hand, when you also look at all the other leading consulting firms, such as Booz & Company, A.T. Kearney, Monitor Group, Towers Perrin, Deloitte Consulting LPP, Roland Berger Strategy Consultants, Accenture and others, there are eventually a considerable amount of consulting positions available each year. For an overview of the leading consulting firms, see Vault's Consulting Firm Rankings: Top 50, which gives a very accurate view of the consulting firm landscape and is freely available online at Vault.com. In the following, a brief overview of the leading consulting companies worldwide is provided, categorized along the type of consulting.

It is important to understand that there are different categories of consulting, with management consulting being probably the most well-known. Other well-known categories of consulting are operations, information technology, and human resources consulting. Some consulting companies specialize in one category; other bigger firms offer consulting services across multiple categories. A last category is the "consulting boutiques". These are the smaller consulting firms, which have a more narrowed scope, and offer limited yet specialized consulting services. It should be noted that there are also the "internal consulting firms," which are basically corporate companies that have incorporated a consulting unit within the organization. This unit focuses on internal consulting jobs, given the corporation's constant need for consulting services.

Understand that working for one of the "best-regarded" consulting companies in the industry does not necessarily mean that firm is the best match for you. When you decide to pursue a career as a consultant, you first need to make up your mind regarding what type of consulting work you would like to do. Second, you should reflect on what you find is important to you in a job. Even though most consulting firms in a particular category are essentially doing the same thing, the way they do things as well as the office atmosphere can differ significantly.

Each of the above described categories, and the leading firms within them, are discussed in more detail in the following. Consulting firms often focus their efforts in one specific category, but often offer other additional consulting services. Additionally the line between these consulting categories is often thin and unclear, for instance aligning the IT infrastructure with the corporate strategy would be considered as IT consulting, but could sometimes also be seen as management consulting.

Management Consulting

Management consulting aims to help organizations enhance their strategic performance. This is primarily realized through the analysis of the client's key strategic challenges. During the assignments, management consultants generally work with the client's senior management. Some of the challenges they address are the following: completing a due diligence process, assisting in mergers and acquisitions, setting the corporate strategy, or renewing an organizational structure.

Traditionally, management consulting firms made their analysis, and completed their assignment with their final recommendations. Nowadays clients on the other hand often expect the consulting firm to realize the implementation of their recommendations, thus increasing the engagement of the firm.

Generally, management consultants have a degree in management, economics, industrial engineering, accounting, or finance. Many leading consulting firms also recruit high-potential candidates with different academic backgrounds, as long as they demonstrate strong business insight.

Some of the most well-known management consulting firms include McKinsey & Company, Bain & Company, and The Boston Consulting Group.

Operations Consulting

Operations consulting, or operational consulting, involves assessing the actual status of a company's internal processes and procedures and improving the overall operational productivity of a company. Some of the most important issues operations consultants address are enhancing procurement, optimizing production processes, operating and inventory costs, and improving customer service. Note that several of the major operations consulting firms now also have a sub branch offering strategy-consulting services.

Operations consulting firms have almost always been involved in the actual implementation of their recommendations. This involvement can both be passive or active. In some cases, consultants remain within the firm managing and following-up the implementation process. In other cases the consultant team might remain available to their client, but not be involved in the day-to-day implementation.

Often operations consultants have a degree in business, management, operations, economics, or industrial engineering. Having said this, operations consulting firms also recruit high-potential candidates from different academic backgrounds, as long as they have demonstrated strong business insight.

Some of the most well-known operations consulting firms include Deloitte Touche Tohmatsu Limited and PricewaterhouseCoopers.

Information Technology Consulting

Overall, two types of information technology (IT) consulting can be distinguished. On one hand, there are the IT consulting firms that focus on the technical issues. On the other hand, there are the IT consulting firms that help organizations manage their business processes to meet their business objectives through IT. Some of the main challenges of IT consulting firms are IT complexity management, alignment of the IT structure with the business objectives, and IT outsourcing.

Although information technology consultants often have a background in computer science, electronics, management of information systems, or technology, these firms often expect their employees to also have strong business intuition or management backgrounds.

Some of the most well-known information technology consulting firms include Booz Allen Hamilton, Tata Consulting Services, and Accenture.

Human Resources Consulting

Human resources (HR) consulting is currently on the upswing, being one of the most fashionable consulting fields. It focuses its efforts on optimizing an organization's most important asset, namely, its people. Over time, clients' labor needs have become more specialized and demanding. Human resources consulting firms are hired to close the gap between a firm's HR needs and its workforce capabilities. Some of the core fields that HR consulting firms specialize in are human capital management, mergers and acquisitions, and HR outsourcing.

HR consultants often have academic backgrounds in business or management. Nevertheless, human resources consulting firms are always on the lookout for talented candidates with strong business intuition.

Some of the leading human resources consulting firms are Mercer Consulting, Hewitt Associates, and Tower Watson.

Boutique Consulting Firms

Boutique consulting firms are consulting firms that focus their services on a small number of industries, business issues, or methodologies. Instead of covering a wide range of consulting services, boutiques dedicate their efforts to a small number of domains in which they build strong expertise. Given this, they are generally smaller than the other types of consulting firms. Even though there are some boutique consulting firms with more than 500 employees, most have 200 or fewer. Notice that these firms are not necessarily less ambitious. Actually, for some specific services, these boutique consulting firms are often more in demand than are the larger firms.

When investigating which consulting firms you want to apply to, it is always interesting to investigate whether there are certain boutique consulting firms specialized in your specific domains of interest. If you find a firm that matches your specific interests, working there would mean that you could spend almost all your time on cases that match your profile, which is clearly more difficult to do within the larger consulting firms.

Some of the most well-known boutique consulting firms include Charles River Associates, L.E.K. Consulting, and Strategic Decisions Group.

BANKING CAREERS

Many graduates also aspire to a career at one of the leading financial corporations, and their main motivations are often obvious. Think about the enormous payroll within the sector for the first year: around $75.000 for new analysts up to $200,000 for investment bankers with MBAs. Furthermore, gaining experience with a leading investment firm can lead to many other career opportunities. Many people who spend some years at an investment bank, or a major financial institution, move on to the top management of a leading corporation. Most jobs in the banking sector are furthermore very high profile, given the media coverage on acquisitions and other deals supervised by banking companies. The work you and your team do could be published in some of the leading financial newspapers. Most jobs in the banking sector are in addition intellectually very challenging and involve intensive training programs.

The first drawback always mentioned within the banking sector is the high amount of working hours. Nonetheless, within the banking sector, significant differences in working hours exist. The leading financial institutions, often referred to as "bulge bracket banks," and the leading boutique banks will often require their employees to work at least 80 hours per week, up to 100 working hours and more. In this case, working all-nighters and on the weekend will become the rule rather than the exception. This will even more be the case if you are based in one of the world's leading financial centers such as New York, London, or Hong Kong. On the other hand, where most positions in the leading banking sector require a considerable number of working hours, you could also start at a less renowned banking company with similar job tasks, but fewer hours. The latter would allow you to have a better lifestyle, but the payroll will obviously be lower. It is interesting to note that most professionals at leading financial institutions say that the biggest drawback is not the long working hours but rather the unpredictability of working hours, which may take its toll on your personal life. You might then ask yourself why financial institutions do not simply hire more staff to do the work. The answer is that is simply part of the banking culture. Banking jobs also generally require less traveling than consulting jobs. It is often only when you reach a more senior position that traveling would become a more important part of the job. Depending on your lifestyle and personal preferences, this could be seen as an advantage or a disadvantage.

Given that the number of employees at banking companies is generally higher relative to consulting companies, there are more positions available in financial institutions. Regardless of that, landing one of the top positions at one of the bulge bracket banks will be very difficult, require an impressive resume and a significant amount of interview preparation. For an overview of the leading financial institutions, go to Vault's Banking Employers Ranking: Top 50. The ranking is based upon prestige, job satisfaction, working hours, compensation package, and firm culture; and it gives a good overview of the leading banking firms. Additionally, the website provides information on each individual company.

CORPORATE CAREERS

Many graduates also consider launching their professional career at one of the major multinational corporations. These firms have in general more positions available and are among the biggest recruiters of MBA students and talented undergraduates.

The main difference with corporate careers relative to consulting or banking careers is that generally you will be working and spending time with people within your organization, which makes a corporate career more internally oriented. Consultants and bankers, on the other hand, are continuously directly delivering services to their clients and are therefore much more externally oriented. This, however, does not necessarily mean that you will never deal with external parties.

In general, corporate careers demand fewer working hours and provide better job security relative to consulting or banking positions. Obviously, the amount of weekly working hours varies from one corporation to another, but weeks of more than 60 working hours will definitely be the exception. On the other hand, corporate careers often have lower starting salaries compared with starting bankers or consultants. Furthermore, most corporate careers require less traveling on the job, which again might be seen as an advantage for some and a drawback by others. It is nonetheless difficult to generalize all corporate multinationals. Compare your profile with the corporate culture of the firm you are considering, to see whether there is a match. You will discover a lot about the company's culture during the interview, but additionally look for online and off-line sources for supplementary information on the working environment and corporate culture of the specific corporation.

Corporate careers can be synonymous with office bureaucracy, more so than consulting or banking careers. Working through a firm's hierarchy and office politics can be frustrating, but these are, however, part of many global corporate organizations. While some corporations are well-known for their office bureaucracy, others are doing all they can to eliminate organizational bureaucracy inefficiencies as much as possible.

The career path is in general more obvious for corporate careers, but you would still have many interesting opportunities. Multinational corporations have, for example, offices in several countries, and international transfers are usually possible if desired. Furthermore, most corporations allow you to switch between business units within one office, and some even allow you to completely change job function through special training programs.

Nowadays, management trainee programs offered by many of the leading multinational corporations are very much in demand by talented graduates. These entry-level programs offer a significant amount of training and generally involve rotating among various positions within the company for some months, allowing you to discover the business unit and role of your preference. This allows you to have a taste of several job positions within the company before deciding on your starting position. These programs often last one to two years and are designed to expedite your career path within the firm.

Some examples of the leading corporations that are looking for the most talented graduates are Nike, Google, Intel, 3M, Microsoft, Procter & Gamble, General Electric, Kraft, and IBM. All these corporations offer exciting and challenging careers, with interesting career perspectives. When considering a corporate career, it would be a good idea to first find out which sector you would prefer to work in, such as for example utilities, consumer goods, electronics, or pharmaceuticals. Then you can look more closely at all the companies within the sectors of your interest and decide where you will apply.

Chapter II

Real-life Interviews

This chapter addresses the most important skills assessed during a case interview. The entire case interview process is explained in greater detail. Each step of the interview process is analyzed individually, and advice on how to be successful in each step is given. You will notice how several small things can have a difference on the eventual outcome of your case interview performance.

SKILLS ASSESSED

In general, most interviewers receive a standard template from the HR department, which they will use to assess your performance during the interview. Understanding what your interviewer will be evaluating you on will obviously make you a better interviewee. For this reason, here is a list of the most important skills/qualities that interviewers will be keeping an eye out for during the case interview.

Analytical Skills

Arguably, the most important consulting skill is your analytical capacity. This essentially encompasses your ability to break down a problem into its smaller parts, your understanding of each part, and eventually using the acquired knowledge to come up with a sensible recommendation or conclusion. You can demonstrate your analytical skills best through a solid understanding of the most important business concepts, logical derivations, and spot-on questions necessary to progress through your case.

Excellence

One of the biggest differences between academic life and professional life probably lies in impeccable excellence. While it is acceptable at university to skip a course, to once have a lower grade, or even to miss a deadline, it is not acceptable in professional life. During your career, excellence in your work will thus always be key. For example incorrectly recommending that a firm should close one of its manufacturing plants would have serious consequences.

During your interview, you can show your working excellence by demonstrating strong quantitative skills and by using a data-driven approach to come to a conclusion. Make sure that your recommendations are backed up by data that prove your point. Often, however, you might not have all the data needed to prove your point fully. When you then have to make a recommendation, make sure that your wording is correct. Two similar statements, such as "The data suggest that…" instead of "The data clearly say that…" have, for instance, very different implications.

Client Skills

Consultants already get in contact with clients at a very early stage. Where client contact is initially with the middle management, you might quickly be sitting with senior managers. Given this, a question most interviewers will be asking themselves is, 'Can we go to the client with this guy?' To demonstrate strong client skills, you need to come across as mature and professional. Therefore, you should be able to present yourself quickly, communicate effectively and correctly, and make sure you come across as honest and humble. Too often, brilliant students come across as arrogant, for which they failed the interview round. Last but not least, to show good client skills, your wording will again be very important. Keep in mind that a correct answer is an answer that is not only accurate, but also client-friendly.

Organizational Skills

Consultants generally have very busy schedules, but they need to be at their best at all times. Therefore, they must consistently be extremely organized and structured. In the interview process, the interviewer will be looking at whether you come across as a well-organized person. To demonstrate that you are well-organized, make sure you are on time for the interview, have a pad of paper and a pen at hand, take legible notes, and communicate in a logical and structured way. Additionally, during the job consultants often get involved in delicate situations under pressure.

Your interviewer, therefore, will want to evaluate your ability to keep your cool during the interview. It is up to you to demonstrate you are calm and have everything under control.

Creativity

Creativity and the ability to think outside of the box are also important consulting skills, and will, thus, be evaluated. Your interviewer might be assessing your ability to identify multiple ways to analyze or structure a problem by suddenly introducing new information that radically alters your current methodology. It is then important for you to demonstrate your flexibility and creativity to work around this problem and to come up with a newly suggested approach.

Personality

Clearly not all consulting firms are the same. Some firms are known to be very competitive; others, more collaborative. Some firms are known to put their employees under serious pressure, whereas others provide a better work/life balance. Many other differences among consulting firms can be thought of. Therefore, every consulting firm clearly has a different working culture. During the interview, your task is to assess whether you would like to work with your interviewer or work for that particular firm. Your interviewer, however, will be doing the same evaluation to assess your fit with the organization. The biggest advice here is to stay true to yourself, and not try to be what you think the consulting firm expects of you.

INTERVIEW PROGRESSION

Interviews at consulting firms almost always have the same structure. Five critical steps in which you will have to perform well to convince the interviewer you are the right person for the job can be identified. The five-steps model, which is presented below, is used to explain in detail the progress of consulting interviews.

Chitchat → About the inverviewer → About yourself → The business case → Questions & Answers

Exhibit 1 - The five-steps interview progression model

Keep in mind that from the moment the interviewer walks in till he leaves the room, you will be evaluated. Every question and every action has a precise reason, namely, to determine whether you are a perfect fit for the consulting firm. Therefore, a detailed understanding of the entire interview process will obviously give you a competitive advantage, as you will appear more confident. Keep in mind that this five-steps model is a general guideline for the progress of most consulting interviews. Nonetheless, some interviewers might take another approach and, for example, skip certain steps.

To get accustomed with this interview process, you should first interview at consulting companies in which you are less interested. From these first interviews, you will learn a lot, without blowing your chances with the companies you are most interested in.

The Chitchat Phase

From the moment an interviewer walks in the room, he or she is already observing you. Several little things will be evaluated immediately, and the reason for this is quite obvious. When you would be a consultant waiting in a client's room, you would also need to make a good impression to your client from the start. Therefore, the interviewer will evaluate whether you make a pleasant and self-confident first impression. Given that a strong start is often key for success, you better make a good impression. The following explains each detail you will have to pay attention to from the start. Practice this phase with other people, and you will become stronger over time. Generally this phase will not take longer than one minute, but depends from interviewer to interviewer.

Offer a firm handshake, a genuine smile, and a simple opener

When your interviewer walks in the room, walk towards him at a normal pace and give him a firm handshake, along with a genuine smile. Furthermore, introduce yourself. You could simply say, "Hi, my name is Robert Johnson; it's really nice to meet you." Remember that this person is in a position that you are applying for, and thus, meeting with him or her should be, by definition, interesting for you. Additionally, look the interviewer in the eyes while you are talking, and also when he or she is talking to you. After your opener, simply walk back to your chair at a normal pace.

Once sitting, make sure you sit in an upright position

Once you sit, adopt a good sitting posture. Make sure you are sitting relatively straight and feel comfortable. You will consequently find your breathing to be better, and you will be more relaxed. Try to maintain this posture throughout the interview. Keep in mind that sitting upright gives a more professional impression and conveys you are confident and at ease during the interview.

Remember your appearance

Have you ever looked around in the office of a consulting firm and noticed how well-groomed most consultants are? The reason behind this is that well-groomed people appear to be more vital, to be better organized, and to have better eye for detail. As a consultant, you need to make several first impressions on the job. For this, it is important to look neat not only at work but also, of course, when going on an interview at the firm. Consulting firms generally expect their consultants to be shaven, have a proper suit and buttoned-up shirt. Furthermore, take the effort to look your best when arriving at the company. This will give yourself more confidence and will be well appreciated by your interviewers.

Show you are happy to be there

First of all, the interviewer has an extremely busy schedule, so you should demonstrate appreciation for him or her making time to interview you. Second, he or she will be evaluating whether you look excited to be there or whether you are just at another consulting firm doing an interview. Simply be friendly and show your respect for the interviewer. You could thank him or her for making time for you, or give a nice comment on the office location or the office's view. The most important thing here is that you mean it; if you don't, your interviewer might notice your insincerity, and that would obviously give you bad points.

Be communicative and open for some small talk

Some interviewers prefer starting immediately; others want to chitchat for a minute. The reason for this chitchat is evident. Clients of consulting companies often also chitchat about whatever topic. The interviewer might evaluate whether or not you are a nice person to have a little small talk with. Therefore, always be ready to talk about topics such as the weather, the office view, or how you came to the office. Some interviewers may have attended the same university and/or exchange program as you have, and will immediately start talking about their experiences. Be prepared to talk about it; share his or her enthusiasm and demonstrate you had great times yourself. Furthermore, some interviewers might be really passionate about a certain subject, such as the Super Bowl, an important soccer game, the media, or whatever. Even if you do not know anything about the topic, show some enthusiasm and be able to at least participate in some small talk about it. In general, your interviewer will eventually take the lead to progress the interview to the next stage.

Develop a ready-to-start mentality

As mentioned, some interviewers enjoy the chitchat phase, but others think it is a waste of time. Therefore, always be ready to start from the moment the interviewer walks in. When the interviewer, for example, walks in and immediately presents him- or herself, or even directly fires a question at you, make sure you are ready to start. At any point when the interviewer indicates the "interview" has started, he is actually saying he wants to move to the next phase. You could then briefly state something like "Of course" or "That is why we are here."

Make sure you have everything you need

Keep in mind that for nearly all interviews, you will need a pad of paper and a pen. Some firms will provide them, but most won't. Having to say you did not bring them will leave a terrible impression. Furthermore, if you do forget it, you will most likely have to do the case without them. Therefore, make sure you have them ready for the interview, preferably in a briefcase, and have them close at hand for when you need them. You could additionally take some graph paper with you, which could be useful when you have a business case for which you have to plot graphs. Generally, you are not supposed to use a calculator during a business case. Some interviewers, however, do give business cases for which a calculator is needed, and assume that their interviewees have brought one. Therefore, having a calculator in your briefcase is recommended. Last, you should always have a copy of your motivation letter and resume with you. Generally the HR department will provide the interviewer with a copy of these two documents, but some interviewers expect their interviewees to have them at hand.

About the Interviewer

In the second stage, the interviewer will briefly introduce him- or herself. Expect this to take about two minutes. Nonetheless, this again will vary from interviewer to interviewer. Also during this time, the interviewer will be evaluating you. Unfortunately, many applicants hardly pay attention in this stage of their case interview, because they are already internally preparing for the business case or curriculum-related questions.

Know who your interviewer is upfront

Many consulting companies give information to you upfront regarding who will be interviewing you, as well as their position in the company. Some consulting firms even send a file with information on your interviewers. Keep in mind that information about who is sitting in front of you can only help you. Sometimes you might find out his or her preferred industries to work in, and then you might expect a business case about this sector. Furthermore, you might find out your interviewer has similar interests, went to the same university, or has similar previous work experiences as you do. If the consulting firm can look up information about you, you could do the same.

Obviously, you can never directly say to your interviewer that you looked up information about him or her. You could, however, put a subject on the table that would likely be of interest to your interviewer, given what you found on the Internet. In addition, you might be able to extract information on what the interviewer appreciates in prospective candidates.

This research prior to your actual interview is referred to as "profiling." You can easily find interesting information through Google, by looking up the name and surname of your interviewer. Generally the most interesting information can be derived from websites such as LinkedIn or Facebook. Additionally, several people within the consulting sector have written articles for newspapers, their employer or a personal blog. Extract the interesting profiling information from various information sources, and try to deduce his personal opinions and beliefs. For each interviewer you profile, you should spend at least 30 minutes doing research. Exhibit 2 provides a guideline you could use to structure this research.

Name:

Personal information:

Gender:

Age:

Country of origin:

Marital Status:

Work experience:

Company & Industry:

Specialisation:

Academic background:

Universities:

Exchange programs:

Articles published:

Hobbies & sports:

Other relevant information:

Exhibit 2 - Interviewer profiling sheet

Ask a question or ask for clarification

When the interviewer is presenting him- or herself, it is very important to show interest in his career. A great way to do this is by asking for clarification while the interviewer presents himself. An example could, for instance, be "So you said you went for an MBA after three years; how did the company support you in that?" This question demonstrates that you are carefully listening to the interviewer and are interested in his career path. The clarification should of course be positive and about something not obvious, of which you are not supposed to know the answer. Again, show enthusiasm while raising this question, and never just ask a question to ask one. On some occasions, your interviewer would say you can ask these questions at the end of the interview, but often, he or she will immediately answer and appreciate your interest.

Show enthusiasm and pay attention

When your interviewer is presenting him- or herself, just be calm, because there is definitely nothing to be nervous about. This phase of the interview is a perfect opportunity to become comfortable with the interview setting. The interviewer will do all the talking, and you only need to sit back, relax, and listen while showing genuine enthusiasm for his or her career path. Clearly you are the main character during the interview, but the interview is still about both of you. Therefore, try to make sure that the interviewer has a good time with you as well. Almost everybody likes to talk about his or her career and ambitions, so allow the interviewer to tell his or her story; you will have plenty of time in the next phases to demonstrate your own skills.

About Yourself

When the interviewer has presented himself and announces it is time to get to know you better, you know the interview is about to progress to the next step of the five-steps interview progression model. From now on, most of the time will be dedicated to profoundly evaluate you and your skills. Nonetheless, as explained, you have already been assessed on several skills. While in the first two stages you are moreover assessed on your social skills set, you will now be assessed on your leadership, entrepreneurial and analytical skills. In general the interviewer will start with some questions along your cover letter or CV, and focus on your fit with the core consultant skills.

Have your core values prepared

Most consulting firms have their core values published on their websites. Typically, for consulting firms, these core values are leadership, creativity, and excellence, or something similar. It is advisable to look up the core values of the firm you are interviewing with, and to know them by heart. Even more important is to have at least one example ready of a time when you showed this particular value in the past. Very often, your interviewer would ask something like "In our company, this value is very important, can you give me a situation in which you have demonstrated this?" Notice that each value has its particular elements that should be included in your explanation. The following list provides a brief overview of some of the most common core values, and some of their respective elements:

- **Leadership:** Strong project management skills, openness, clear vision, motivational skills, and effective distribution of the work
- **Creativity:** A quicker, a better or an alternative solution to a relevant problem
- **Excellence:** Respect for the quality/accurateness of work

The interviewer is not expecting you to have organized the Super Bowl or to have invented the mobile phone. Just make sure you have your best personal example ready and are able to explain why and how your example demonstrates that particular skill.

List 10 key projects you have accomplished

Before going to an interview, brainstorm the ten most important projects you have accomplished during your life so far. Think about your participation in sports clubs and societies, your personal projects, your academic career path, your professional experiences and so on. Then think about the most important things you have realized there as a team or by yourself, and write it down. Cut down your list to about 10 projects in case you had more examples. Make sure you have both individual and team projects on your list, because it is important to show that you can work by yourself, but it is at least as important to demonstrate you are a team player. Now memorize each project to make sure that if the interviewer asks a question for which you do not have an answer immediately ready, you can use this list to find an appropriate example. Note that the interviewer does not expect you to answer his or her questions right away. It is perfectly fine to take a few seconds to think about your answer.

Know your curriculum vitae and cover letter

Generally, when the interviewer starts asking questions about you, he or she will start with questions on your cover letter and curriculum vitae (CV). In most cases, the interviewer will have received these documents from the HR responsible. Nonetheless, you should always have some copies readily available, because in some cases, the interviewer might ask you whether you have brought these documents with you for him to use it. Generally however, the interviewer has already taken the time upfront to quickly go through your resume and cover letter, and has highlighted some topics he would like to know more about. Make sure you know every line of your curriculum vitae by heart, why you included it, as well as what you wrote in your cover letter. Be prepared upfront to talk about everything you have written there, and note that the most important things on your CV and in your cover letter will be asked about the most. Furthermore, interviewers sometimes ask about what you are most proud of on your CV; make sure you have an answer prepared for this question as well.

Prepare for critical questions

Some questions just tend to come back all the time during interview rounds. For this, it is important to have your best answer ready to make the best possible impression. Nonetheless, you should always make sure your answer never feels "premade"; it should sound natural and fluent. The following is a list of questions that have a much higher-than-average probability of being asked when interviewing at a consulting firm. Note that your interviewer might ask variations of these questions.

Motivation

- Why do you want to be a consultant?
- Why do you want to work for our firm?

Problem-solving skills and creativity

- Describe a situation you handled creatively.
- Describe a situation in which you had to convince others that your approach was right or appropriate.
- Describe a tough problem and how you solved it.

Personal impact

- In your experience with team work, what was your role and impact, and what difficulties occurred?
- Describe your relationships in a working context; how do you work effectively, and how do you solve conflicts?
- Describe a delicate situation in which your personal sensitivity made a difference.

Leadership

- Describe a situation where you recognized a problem/opportunity as well as your response (actions and organization). Which obstacles occurred and how did you overcome them?
- What leadership roles have you played?
- Have you ever had a goal to achieve that required actions by others?

Drive/aspirations

- Where do you want to be in five years?
- Describe a situation where you were aspiring to reach a goal and how you reached it.
- Describe a situation that demanded unusually hard work and how you handled this.

Have one or two negative things about yourself ready

Another popular question is when interviewers ask you to tell something you would like to change about yourself, or an area for improvement you might have. Clearly you should never say you would not change anything about yourself. This question is nonetheless rather tricky, and is one that should definitely be thought about before being interviewed. Try first to identify some skills that you feel you could be better at. These areas for improvement should preferably not be analytical or leadership related, given how important these are for a consulting position. Furthermore speak of the weakness as an opportunity for improvement; say how you will improve this particular skill in the near future or how you could potentially tackle this weakness.

The Business Case

The business case is generally by most interviewees considered the biggest challenge. This phase is often the longest phase of all five (ranging from 20 minutes for a short business case to 45 minutes for a longer business case). It is this part of the interview you will need to prepare the most to really succeed your interview. Studying intensively for the business case part of the interview can help you outperform yourself and others. The following covers what you should and should not do in this particular phase of the interview. The discussion of how to conceptualize and structure business cases effectively can be found in the next chapter. Notice that in this phase the interviewer is mainly trying to assess how structured and analytical you are in your problem solving.

Structure, structure, structure...

The most important thing is to demonstrate to the interviewer your ability to structure your thoughts. Set out a clear structure to solve the problem from the start, and clearly communicate this methodology to your interviewer. Furthermore, it is strongly advised you confirm from the start whether he or she finds your approach appropriate for the business case. You could do this by saying, "Now, if you agree with this approach, I suggest we start our analysis." In case the interviewer believes this approach could be used to crack the case, he or she will confirm this, and you can progress with solving the business case. In case the interviewer does not agree with your approach, you could suggest another methodology or ask what his objections are. It could also happen that the interviewer goes in a completely different direction after you presented your methodology to analyze the case, for instance, by presenting a new document. Notice that this does not necessarily mean that your interviewer does not like your suggested approach.

No industry background is required

Often, candidates have failed because they did not understand the industry in which the business case is situated. This should however never be a reason to fail a business case. No specific industry background is required to crack a business case. If you do not know the particular industry of your business case, for instance, the reinsurance industry, you simply state after the interviewer presented his case, "How exactly does the reinsurance industry work? This, just to be sure I fully understand the context of the case." Unless the industry context is evident, you might want to ask more background information on it. Never start your analysis before understanding the industry you are dealing with.

Take notes

Unless your interviewer states the contrary, you are always allowed to take notes during a business case. In fact, you should take notes. As mentioned, make sure you brought enough paper, preferably with lines, which appears more structured, as well as a working pen. Furthermore you should take a marker to the interview. This allows you to highlight some data, which will help the interviewer to better focus on what is important in your analysis. Make sure you have your pen, pad of paper, and marker close to you when the interview starts so that you do not have to look for it when the interviewer wants to start with the business case.

Think aloud

During the business case, you are supposed to think aloud, as your interviewer wants to see whether you think in a logical and structured way. To become more structured in your analysis, you will need to continuously exercise business cases, and with time you will start to notice your progress. Talk however at a normal pace, or even slightly slower than normal. This will make you appear calm and under control during the analysis.

Leave time for intervention, and listen to your interviewer

Many interviewees try to rush through the business case and ignore the remarks of their interviewer. Often, however, your interviewer will give you tips or hints on the direction you should be going during the business case. By ignoring these "free" clues, you will make the business case more difficult to yourself, and also leave a bad impression. Keep your ears open for all remarks from your interviewer, and see him as your co-pilot who will guide you through the business case. Furthermore, make sure you leave space for intervention. Generally your interviewer has a case in mind and knows where he or she wants you to go. Of course, you cannot read his or her mind and predict this; therefore, your interviewer will intervene wherever needed to make the case go more or less as planned. For this, always let your interviewer finish what he or she wants to say and make sure you understand what your interviewer expects from you.

During your interview, your interviewer might also suggest which areas he or she wants you to address first; make sure you follow this advice. If he or she does not indicate a preference, you could always state, "I will start my analysis with concept A, unless you have a particular preference for where I should first focus on?" Your interviewer might say that you can start as you have suggested; he or she might additionally ask you why you want to start with that in particular, or might suggest you to start with something else. As you can see, working like this continuously leaves space for your interviewer to intervene and keep you on the right track. Create enough of these "opportunities" to make sure you keep on the right track.

Study, study, study…

The best advice that can be given is to practice and study as many business cases as possible. The more you practice cracking business cases, the better you will become at it. Each business case is unique, and you will need as much experience as possible upfront to feel comfortable during the actual interviews.

Questions and Answers

The last five minutes of the interview are generally reserved for you to ask questions. This is your time to better understand your personal fit with the company. After all, you are also there to see whether you would actually like to work for that specific consulting firm. Nonetheless, you will also be evaluated in this phase. The interviewer will be assessing whether you seem passionate and excited for the position. The questions asked, also demonstrate some of your personality. For example, an interviewee asking for the opportunities to do an MBA after some years, demonstrates he or she sees a career at the firm over several years. The questions you ask will leave a certain impression, and therefore, preparing your questions to some extent is recommended.

Furthermore, this phase of the interview can to some extent be used to check whether your interviewer liked the interview with you. If the interviewer has enjoyed interviewing you, he or she will generally not mind spending some extra time answering your questions. In the other case, your interviewer's answers might be shorter, and he or she might be less willing to spend extra time on all your questions. Nonetheless, keep in mind that it is very much possible that your interviewer has another appointment right after your interview, and has to finish the interview even though he or she is very satisfied with your performance. Keep in mind that it is recommended that you never ask your interviewer his or her opinion on how you did during the interview. If you did well, your interviewer would still have to discuss your performance afterwards with the other interviewer(s). If you didn't do well, your interviewer does not want to end up in a situation in which you end up arguing about your performance during the interview.

Prepare some interesting questions in advance

At the time of the interview, interviewees often forget some of the questions they really wanted to ask. To keep this from happening, make a short list of interesting questions for which you definitely would like answers. Memorize these questions, and ask them at the end of the interview. Given that you generally only have five minutes for questions, make sure you start with your most important questions first.

Listen to the answers

Some interviewees hardly listen to their interviewers' answers, but instead, they are already thinking about their next question. Clearly, you would not make a good impression. When you ask your question, always pay attention to your interviewer's reply. It is perfectly fine to ask your interviewer an additional question while he is replying, but in the end, your interviewer should do most of the talking at this stage.

Ask relevant questions

Always take the position of your interviewer into account when asking questions. Asking questions about the firm's strategic vision for the next five years to a senior associate consultant makes less sense than asking the same question to a manager or a partner of the firm. Similarly, a manager or a partner might be less aware of the office activities for which asking a senior associate consultant or a consultant may be better. Furthermore, avoid asking obvious questions and questions for which you can easily find the answer online.

Examples of good questions

Typical questions you would ask to a senior associate consultant or a consultant:

- What would be my main responsibilities during my early assignments?

- What would be the three best tips you could give to a starting (associate) consultant?
- What would a typical week as an (associate) consultant look like?
- How is the contact with the managers and the partners?
- Which skill-building tools and/or training is provided within the firm?
- How many nationalities are present in this office?

Typical questions you would ask to a manager or a partner:

- How would you describe the firm's management style?
- How would you describe a strong performing (associate) consultant?
- What is currently the most pressing business issue or strategic challenge for the firm?
- What have you liked most about working for this consulting firm?
- What would be the three best tips you could give to a new (associate) consultant?
- Which position did you enjoy the most during your career (in case the interviewer went through all or most of the ranks)?

Thank the interviewer for his or her time

At the end of the interview, you should always thank your interviewer for his or her time. You could additionally point out that you enjoyed the business case or the interview in general, if that was the case. Some books even recommend sending an e-mail after the interview to thank your interviewers, though it is generally better to thank the interviewer immediately and in person. Furthermore, in case the interviewer did not mention when you will be contacted with feedback, then you should now ask when you will hear back from the company and who will be contacting you.

Chapter III

How to Crack Your Business Case

The focus in this chapter is on how to crack business cases. It starts by explaining what a business case is, why consulting firms use them in the interview process, and what essentially makes a business case analysis successful. The next part discusses in detail the standard methodology to approach business cases. Then the most important frameworks to assess business cases are discussed, with several examples for each type of framework. The chapter ends with a list of the top ten tips to achieve business case success.

INTRODUCTION TO BUSINESS CASES

What Is a Business Case and Why Is it used?

A business case is an interactive simulation of a business problem. Your task is to structure and analyze the problem by asking logical questions to your interviewer to eventually come up with a detailed, generally data-driven, recommendation.

The reason business cases are put into practice is that consulting firms are aware that the resumes they receive are often only a simple representation of a complex person. Given a consultant's turbulent working environment, a defined personality and a select set of leadership skills are required to be successful. To ensure consulting firms hire the right people, they introduced the business case, which has evolved as a precise method for evaluating these skills. It helps the interviewer to screen candidates and to determine who really has what it takes to become a successful consultant. As mentioned before, your final evaluation will depend on several factors, but your performance on the business case will always have a significant weight in the final outcome.

Different Types of Business Cases

Several types of business cases can be distinguished, generally with different levels of difficulty. The most common types of business cases are the cost/revenue cases, business-situation cases, merger and acquisition cases, and value chain cases, which probably account for about ninety-five percent of the cases. Some interview preparation books additionally consider the guesstimate, which is discussed in chapter five, as a type of business case. In this book, however, the guesstimate is not considered as such, since it is much easier and more mechanical than real business cases.

The level of difficulty of the business case you will receive strongly depends on your background, but it can also be somewhat random. The expectations for undergraduates are for instance lower than those for MBA or advanced degree candidates. Undergraduates tend to receive more guesstimates, cost/revenue cases, or the more straightforward business-situation cases. MBA or advanced degree holders on the other hand are more likely to receive the more difficult business cases. Additionally, the cases given to undergraduates tend to concern less complex industries and firms. Therefore, undergraduates are, for instance, more likely to get a case about a small firm in the beer industry rather than a case on a private equity firm that wants to acquire a company in the reinsurance industry. In case you do get a business case sited in a complex industry or firm, you should, as mentioned, spend some extra time from the start with your interviewer to better understand the dynamics of the firm and its industry. You should, however, never panic, or believe that you cannot crack the case because of the industry context. Once you understand the business case context, all cases essentially consist of breaking down the problem along an appropriate framework and synthesizing the insights into good recommendations.

What Your Interviewer Is Looking For

To know what makes a good business case analysis, it is important to understand the mind-set of the interviewer and have a general understanding of which characteristics he will be looking for. Obviously your interviewer will be assessing your overall performance along multiple dimensions during the business case. There are, however, certain skills that will weigh more in the final evaluation.

The first, and by far the most important, skill you have to demonstrate is process excellence. You should make yourself comfortable with a repeatable and logical process to crack business cases. You should, however, not completely rely on the business frameworks that you studied in advance. You will often need to change the framework to some extent to adjust it to the specific business problem, given that all business cases are different. Practice sufficiently, using the approaches to tackle business cases described later. Ending up with a wrong answer while using a correct approach is better than having the right answer while using a wrong approach. You definitely do not want your interviewer to have the impression that you got lucky with the business case. In addition, keep in mind that knowing how to approach business cases is not the same as being able to consistently crack them. The difference between both lies in a little real-life practice, but the impact on your eventual performance evaluation is enormous.

Second, it is important to continuously be analytical and data-driven, and to follow a linear and logical approach. During your analysis and synthesis, it is thus important that you include and structure all of the relevant pieces of information provided to you.

The last key skill is the ability to synthesize all your findings, to pull together the big picture, and eventually to present your findings coherently. Some people are more talented with this, but through practicing several business cases, you will get a good feeling of how to do this.

Along these three key skills, you will also be evaluated on other skills, such as presentation skills, enthusiasm, and creativity. Notice that having specific knowledge of the case's industry can be a bonus, but it is never required.

It is important to mention here that some interviewers might give you the impression that they are hardly paying attention. They might, for instance, look uninterested, repeatedly check their watch, or even start playing with their smart phone. They do this to see whether you are able to remain calm and maintain focus on the business case. Therefore, stay confident, keep your enthusiasm, and continue solving the case.

How to Practice Business Cases

When you start practicing business cases, the first thing you should do is get accustomed to the standard approach for cracking business cases and the different frameworks. Once you start to feel comfortable with these, it is time to start practicing actual business cases. You can find several examples of interesting business cases on the websites of leading consulting firms. Additionally, you could find interesting business cases examples in other books on case interviews. If you eventually run out of business cases, you could still create them yourself, a methodology to do this is described at the end of this chapter.

Practicing business cases on your own is definitely a great way to start. Unfortunately, you will never have the interaction that you would have in a real-life case interview. While practicing business cases on your own can be quite challenging, doing one aloud with someone else is even more challenging. Therefore, it is advised that at some point, you pair up with classmates, colleagues, or friends to actively practice business cases.

The interviewer should understand the business case in advance and be ready to guide the interviewee throughout the case. The interviewee should never read through the case ahead of time. Always take the business case simulations seriously, and stay close to the actual case interview format. As a last hint, it is recommended that you tape record the business case simulations to afterwards identify potential areas for improvement.

HOW TO APPROACH YOUR BUSINESS CASE

As mentioned before, there are different types of business cases. Each type has a specific framework to solve the problem, and these are explained in detail later on in this chapter. Irrelevant of the type of business case, the overall approach you take during a case interview will, however, always be the same. The only difference at some point will be the type of framework you use, and the questions you ask to your interviewer. I like to refer to this general approach as the "three-steps process."

The idea behind the three-steps process is that you first open the case, then you analyze it, and ultimately you conclude the case. Within each of these three steps is a subset of smaller steps. By chronologically going through each individual step of the approach, you will be able to solve business cases easily in a structured manner. The three-steps process is represented in Exhibit 3.

OPENING	ANALYZING	CLOSING
Collect all initial information.	Initiate the framework.	Synthesize the key case insights.
Verify your understanding of the case.	Assess the framework through specific questions.	Present the "big picture," and back it up with your findings.
Identify the appropriate framework.	Identify all major problem drivers.	Provide the recommendation or next steps.
Draw out and explain the framework.	Advance the framework.	

Exhibit 3 - The three-steps process to approach business cases

By making this process your own and consistently applying it, you will be able to structure the most complex business cases. Each of these three steps is discussed into detail in the following. Keep in mind that this is a general approach, applicable to most business cases. You might, however, come across a business case where you are not presumed to precisely follow this chronological approach. The majority of these steps will nevertheless recur, but at times, your interviewer might require you to skip certain steps to maintain the dynamics of the business case. For example, you might present a perfectly correct framework, after which your interviewer gives you a new document with all actual problem drivers. If this is the case, be flexible, adjust yourself to the new situation, and continue solving the business case.

Opening

Collect all initial information

To start your business case, first ensure that you have a pad of paper and a pen in front of you. Once your interviewer starts explaining the specifics of the business case, write down all the (potentially) relevant information. Even certain little details might end up being important at a later stage in the case, and you definitely do not want to miss these. While it is better to write too much than too little, you should neither literally write down everything your interviewer says. Just make sure you are able to grasp all the interesting facts and figures of which you feel might be relevant later on. If, at some point, certain information is not clear or ambiguous, make sure to write it down and underline it. In this stage it is however advised to not interrupt your interviewer while he is explaining the business case. While some interviewers would not mind you doing this, others might get annoyed.

Verify your understanding of the case

Once your interviewer has finished presenting the business case, you should take some time to see whether everything is clear to you. Unless your interviewer has been very generous in explaining you all the facts of the case, you will probably still have some specific questions. You should definitely ensure that you have understood all the information provided and that you precisely know what you are expected to analyze and evaluate. Even if you are convinced that you understand the content of the business case, confirming some information with your interviewer to make sure you indeed do is smart. You might, for instance, need to confirm certain figures or require some further explanation to better understand the industry context of the business case. Additionally, if in the previous step, you underlined certain information that was unclear, now will be the time to ask further information. Keep in mind, however, that you should definitely not yet dive into the case by starting to ask very specific questions.

Identify the appropriate framework

The next step during the opening is to identify the appropriate framework to analyze the business case, and this is probably one of the most critical steps. Tell your interviewer you would like a minute to determine the most suitable framework for the case. Make use of this time to identify the best framework, given the information, and start thinking on how you would tackle the case. Keep in mind that this is an internal process, and you should thus be thinking about this on your own. Often your interviewer will quickly go for a coffee or answer an email on his smart phone, don't worry this is completely normal. Once you are ready, just indicate you are prepared to move on.

To know which problems relate to which frameworks, refer to the next two sections that cover the different types of business cases together with several examples. Often, it will be quite clear from the information provided which framework would be the most suitable. Only by continuously practicing business cases, however, will you be able to really perfect your sense of which framework to use. Make sure, that you are flexible with your framework, since specific information that you receive during the business case might require adjustments in the framework. It is good to have a framework to start with, but you should, however, never squeeze the business case in your framework. Use the most appropriate framework and be open for adjustments and new directions of analysis.

Draw out and explain the framework

Now that you have identified the most appropriate framework, it is time for you to draw it out and explain it briefly to your interviewer. Make sure that your framework is readable and that it is flexible for changes. Also consider whether it would be easier to draw it out as landscape or as portrait. I advise you to move closer to your interviewer once you start explaining your framework. It is a great way to engage your interviewer in your analysis, and you will appear much more collaborative.

Do not go into too much detail when explaining your framework, but make sure your interviewer understands the structure you want to follow. Furthermore, you should never actually name your framework. Your interviewer knows the most important frameworks, and will assume you know them as well. Keep in mind that naming your framework might come across as too academic.

Before you start analyzing the case, it is important that you confirm your proposed framework with your interviewer. Often, your interviewer will approve your suggested framework, which generally means your framework should be able to identify the most important issues. It does happen that the interviewer confirms your framework even though it will likely not help you with identifying the major issues. Interviewers do this mainly to assess whether you are able to realize that you are not using an appropriate or correct framework. What also occasionally happens is that the interviewer brings in a new piece of information that makes your proposed framework less usable. The reason interviewers do this, is to assess whether you are flexible and able to manage a small change of course. For the same reason, some interviewers propose you use another framework, even though the one you have selected is perfectly fine. Given this, you can never really conclude anything from your interviewer's approval or disapproval of your proposed framework. Your intuition as to how well the framework will perform and is performing while analyzing the business case will be of the utmost importance. Again the only way to get this intuition is by continuously practicing.

Analyzing

Initiate the framework

The concept of analyzing means breaking down a problem into its smaller parts and assessing them together with their interrelationships. When initiating the analysis of your framework, the first question is where you should start the analysis. All frameworks consist of different blocks or branches, and often in business cases, the key issue you have to solve relates to only one or two particular blocks within the framework. You should try to start the analysis where you think it is most important, that is, where you think there is the highest chance to find an important issue. For this reason, the first thing you should do when initiating your framework is ask your interviewer whether any information from the client might suggest where to start. Generally your interviewer will give you 'no' for an answer. He or she will, however, recognize the value of this question, as it could have saved you a considerable amount of time. In case he or she does provide you a hint on where to start the analysis, there are usually two possibilities. One possibility is that the business case is rather large, and to save time, your interviewer decided to put you on the right track. Another possibility is that your interviewer puts you on the wrong track to test whether you are able to realize this, and move on to the next part of the framework. In each case, you should follow the track suggested by your interviewer. Just be skeptical, as he or she might be testing you.

In case your interviewer did not give any hint where to start the analysis, you could start with the first branch of the framework. It is however recommended, as mentioned before, that you attempt to begin the analysis where you might expect the problem drivers to be situated. The best way to do this is by briefly stating an assumption on where to start best, and preferably, with your reasoning behind it. Examples of assumptions are, for instance, "I will first look at the revenues side, as costs for service companies are often rather low" or "I will first assess the competition, as competition in the airline industry is quite fierce," but simply saying, "I suggest that I first have a look at our client's product" is also perfectly fine. As you will see in the next step, you will need to go through the framework and gather data to assess whether your assumption was correct. In case your assumption was off, you could state another assumption and evaluate that one.

Assess the framework through specific questions

Once you have decided in which branch of the framework you will start, begin by asking the standard questions specific to that framework. These standard questions are discussed into detail further on, in the section on different types of business case frameworks. If, on one hand, the interviewer's answers seem to confirm your initial assumption, you can dive deep until you identified the main issues within that branch of the framework. If, on the other hand, you don't seem to discover anything surprising, you should not be hesitant to move to another branch. When this is the case, indicate to your interviewer that you feel you have collected enough information on that particular part of the framework and that you will move on to a next branch of the framework. Always keep in mind that while your interviewer is answering these standard questions, you should always write down his answers.

Identify all major problem drivers

When you discover a problem driver, it is smart to ask your interviewer whether this accounts for most of the client's problems or whether it is a minor issue. In case your interviewer indicates that the issue you identified is not a major problem driver, it is smart to simply underline the issue. Then indicate to your interviewer that you will continue the analysis to identify other problem drivers and address it later on. If the interviewer, however, states that the issue has a major stake in the overall problem, you might want to start addressing it directly, as it would have the biggest impact. You could also quickly finish the other branches of the framework and possibly identify some other minor issues, but if your interviewer insists you to focus your efforts on that major issue, it is time to go to the next step.

In case you went through the entire framework and you feel you might still be missing something, you could ask your interviewer whether he or she has any other issues he would want to consider. In case you did forget something, your interviewer would likely give you a hint on what you are missing. If your interviewer says you covered all the major issues, you are ready to go to the next step.

Before you start "advancing the framework," as described in the next step, it is a good idea to briefly list the problem drivers that you identified, as well as how critical each one likely is to the client's problem.

Advance the framework

Advancing the framework, which means refining the analysis to identify the "real" insights, is often seen as the most challenging step in the business case. To advance the framework, you will have to continuously refine the framework, or switch to another framework to find those key insights. It is often here that you can make the biggest difference by practicing multiple business cases in advance.

In smaller business cases, the focus might be more on the first three steps of the analyzing part of the three-steps process, in which you are asked to cover the entire framework and identify the major problem drivers. In longer business cases, however, the interviewer will generally push you to profoundly advance the framework and to identify deeper insights about the case. Depending on both the type of business case and how efficient you were in the previous three steps, you might end up rather quickly or late to this stage of the analysis.

Once you have identified all the issues, you should first reflect on which of these are the most important. It is there that you should focus your further analysis, as that will have the biggest impact. Usually in the previous step, you will already be given a suggestion on where to focus. If not, you could now ask the interviewer whether he or she has a preference on which problem drivers you should address first.

Now that you decided how to move on, quickly reflect on a structured approach to fully understand the particular issues. The most important is that you completely understand why these problems occur and what can be done about it. For example, you might have identified three problem drivers, with the major one being that a key competitor has cut prices three months ago by 15 percent, which has had an enormous impact on the client's sales. You now first need to find out how this is possible, and secondly what the client can do about it. You might ask the interviewer for more information on the cost structure of the client and the competitor, or maybe for information on the competitor's recent major activities (maybe the competitor realized serious economies of scale or a vertical integration). Many other questions could be thought of, depending on the type of business case. The most important is that you structure the questions as logically as possible and that you keep asking relevant questions until you have a complete understanding of the problem drivers. It is suggested that while you are refining your analysis, you constantly draw out your refined structure. The reason is that these visuals make your reasoning easier for the interviewer to follow, which is eventually in your advantage. Once you have fully analyzed and understood the major problem drivers, it is time to wrap up your analysis and start closing the business case.

Closing

Synthesize the key case insights

The first thing you need to do to close a case is briefly synthesizing all the insightful pieces of the analysis. This means combining the individual conclusions and putting them together as a coherent whole. This coherent whole eventually is a summary of what the situation/opportunity is, and thus shows "the big picture." This synthesis will eventually be of most value to the client.

Present the big picture and back it up with your findings

Once you have understood the bigger picture, it is time to present your findings in a logical and client friendly way. One great method to do this is described in the book *The Pyramid Principle* by Barbara Minto, who worked several years for McKinsey & Company. She suggests, in her book, that you first present the one key insight of the case and then provide the two to three most relevant pieces of data that support this vision. Sometimes, however, you might end up with multiple key insights, in which case you present each main insight separately, together with its most important supporting data. One simple illustration of the this principle could, for instance, be "Our client should enter the Australian market, because of the following three reasons: the market size is attractive, the market growth is staggering, and our client's product offer is superior to all competitors." As you can observe, this way of presenting your findings will make it easy for the interviewer to follow your conclusion.

Provide the recommendation or next steps

Once you have explained the big picture, supported by strong arguments, your interviewer might ask you to come up with a recommendation or with subsequent steps. In case he or she does not, and you feel you have some good suggestions, you could take the lead and suggest a course of action based upon the business case insights. Always keep in mind that your recommendation should be a logical consequence of the analysis and synthesis.

Often candidates tend to come up with a recommendation that is theoretically correct but practically not always feasible. Keep in mind that your suggested actions should be realistic and preferably not just a theoretical construct. Recommending, for instance, to Microsoft that they should close down a department with fifty employees would be realistic; laying off 10,000 people on the other hand not. In case you would find out that a department with 10,000 employees is unprofitable and has poor future prospects, you could suggest revenue-enhancing or cost-cutting programs, or maybe even selling off that department.

To get a good feeling of which recommendations to make, previous professional experience is probably a good guide. If you, however, do not yet have that experience, you could start reading business cases on alarming business situations to learn from the described course of actions taken. One great source for business cases is the *Harvard Business Review*.

Last, it is important to pay attention to your wording when making your recommendation. If you collected a considerable amount of data to prove a point, you can be rather confirmative. You could for instance say, "Given the data, it is quite clear that our client should target the Australian market." If you, however, have insufficient data to substantiate your recommendation, you might need to be more suggestive. You could then for instance say, "Given the data, our client should likely enter the Australian market, but further analysis would be needed to confirm this." The difference between both recommendations is without a doubt considerable. Where the first one proposes immediate action, the other one suggests realizing additional analysis.

DIFFERENT TYPES OF BUSINESS CASE FRAMEWORKS

Numerous types of business situations could be imagined. Luckily the set of frameworks to tackle most is rather small. More specifically, four frameworks are covered here that will enable you to tackle about all business cases.

It happens that to tackle certain business cases, you need to switch from one framework to another, often to advance the analysis. Once you are comfortable with the different types of frameworks, they become straightforward, and you will notice that you will become more flexible in using them. In the following, all the frameworks are discussed one by one, after which a series of examples of these frameworks is provided.

The Internal Profit-Problem Framework

The internal profit-problem framework is the easiest framework of all four. It is the most mechanical and straightforward, and is in general used to identify one of the following three types of client problems:

- An increase in costs
- A decrease in revenues
- A decrease in profit margin

The first thing you always have to do when an interviewer presents a case where a client has one of these problems, is ask whether this is an industry-wide phenomenon or rather unique to the client. Neglecting this could result in you using the wrong framework. If the profit problem is client related, you should use the internal profit-problem framework to evaluate the situation. In case the problem is industry-wide, however, you should rather use the business-situation framework.

Before illustrating and explaining the internal profit-problem framework, it is important to familiarize yourself with the following formulas:

Profit = Revenues - Costs,

where **Revenues** = Σ (Volume sold per product × Sales price per product), and **Costs** = (Fixed Costs) + Σ (Production volume per product × Variable Unit Cost per product). Modeling this formula in a framework will give us the internal profit-problem framework:

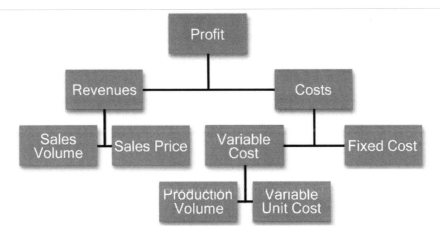

Exhibit 4 - The internal profit-problem framework

Once you presented the framework to your interviewer, remember to ask whether the client sells one or multiple products. If this is the case, you should always ask for the segmented data per product or product category. It is, for instance, possible that overall profits are increasing except for one particular product category. By segmenting per product, or product category, you can quickly identify this type of issue and immediately focus your analysis on that specific product or product category.

The idea behind the framework is that you break down the total profit into its smaller components, using a structured top-down approach. You then rigorously have to question your interviewer how all the elements of the framework changed over time and why. By doing so, you will obtain the necessary information to know whether you should further investigate a branch or should exclude it from additional analysis. This will eventually allow you to identify the root cause of the profit problem. To realize this, you ask for example your interviewer whether profits went down because of a decrease in revenues or an increase in costs. Let us say that a decrease in revenues drove the drop in profits; then you should subsequently ask whether this is due to a decrease in sales volume or a decrease in sales price for the product(s). Keep in mind, however, that there might be multiple drivers for the profit problem. It could be, for instance, a combination of a decrease in revenues and an increase in costs.

Once you get familiar with the framework, you will notice that it does not have to take much time to identify the problem drivers. When you have identified them, your interviewer may ask you to already come up with actionable recommendations to tackle the profit issue or may ask you to deepen your analysis by advancing the framework. A common transition here is from the internal profit-problem framework to the business-situation framework, which is explained next. You might, for example, have identified that revenue has fallen because of a decrease in sales volume and be asked to further analyze what has happened. You could then shift to the business-situation framework and start analyzing the product pillar, to maybe find out that the latest product change was not really appreciated by the customers. Similarly, for business cases where profits increased slower than the industry average, the profit-problem framework will often be a good start, but again, you will likely have to shift to the business-situation framework.

The Business-Situation Framework

The idea behind the business-situation framework is that most high-level issues are generally customer, product, client or competition related. Therefore, to understand any business situation, it is key to first get a good understanding of these four important areas. To this extent, several business concepts, such as Porter's five forces or the 4 P's, are integrated into the business-situation framework.

The business-situation framework is eventually a very broad framework and is generally used to tackle the more strategic business cases. The following is a selection of different business problems for which this framework is used:

- Responding to a competitor's actions
- Moving into an adjacency/new business
- Corporate (growth) strategy
- Entering a new market
- Launching a new product
- Business performance analysis

The only difference between these different business problems is where in the business-situation framework you would start your analysis. In a business case on launching a new product, you would likely start your analysis with the product or the customer. In a business case on responding to a competitor's actions, on the other hand, you would likely start your analysis with the competition. If you are not sure where to begin the analysis, it is often a good idea to start with the customer, as the customer ultimately drives what is going on in the marketplace. Additionally, when you are not sure which framework to use for a rather strategic business case, it is often smart to start by default with the business-situation framework.

First, a general overview of the business-situation framework is given, which is more or less what you would draw out when explaining the framework during the business case interview. Next, all the separate elements of the framework are discussed in further detail. Notice that you can always extend the business-situation framework, depending on the specifics of the business case, by integrating additional relevant questions or business concepts within the four pillars of the framework.

CUSTOMER	PRODUCT	CLIENT	COMPETITORS
Segments and characteristics Key needs Buying power	Specifics and segmentation Commodity/ differentiation Complements and substitutes Product life cycle Packaging	Core capabilities and adjacencies Revenue and cost structure Organizational structure Financial situation	Industry concentration and market share Competitive behavior Entry barriers Regulations

CUSTOMER

Segments and characteristics:
- Which customer segments exist and what are their relative market spendings?
- Which segments are most profitable, and which ones are growing fastest?
- Which customer segments does our client target? (past & present)

Key needs:
- Are there specific different customer needs per segment? Is our client meeting his customers' needs? Are there differences in preferred distribution channels per segment?

Buying power:
- Are customers dispersed, or do a couple of customers control the demand?

PRODUCT (OR SERVICE)

Specifics and segmentation:
- Which different product segments exist? Which products/services is our client selling?
- What are the characteristics of these products/services, and how does it work?

Commodity/differentiation:
- Is the product a commodity or is it differentiated? Is further differentiation possible?

Complements and substitutes:
- Are there many complements or substitutes to our client's products/services?

Product life cycle:
- In which stage of the product life cycle are the products/services? Are new products being developed?

Packaging:
- How are the products packaged? (Differentiation, combined sales,...?)

CLIENT (COMPANY)

Core capabilities and adjacencies:
- In which businesses is our client, and which are our client's core competencies?
- In which adjacencies is our client involved?

Revenue and cost structure:
- How have revenues and costs evolved over time relative to the competitors? (profit problem?)
- What is the cost per unit relative to competitors, and how did this evolve? (best practice)

Organizational structure:
- How are our client's suppliers concentrated? Have there been any recent operational issues?
- Which investments did/does our client make, and which distribution channels are used?

Financial situation:
- Is our client financially healthy? Does our client have large cash reserves?

COMPETITORS (INDUSTRY)

Industry concentration and market share:
- How is the industry structured? (monopoly, oligopoly,...)
- How are the market shares distributed and how did they evolve? What is our client's share?

Competitive behavior:
- On what is competition mainly based? (price, quality,...)
- Have competitors changed their strategy recently?

Entry barriers:
- How are the entry barriers in the industry? (high fixed costs?)
- Have there recently been new entrants?

Regulations:
- Are there specific important regulations within the industry?

Exhibit 5 - The business-situation framework and its sub-components

Depending on the specifics of the business case, you might have to leave out certain questions. Reasons could be that the answer is obvious, or because they are not relevant to the particular company or its industry. If you, for example, have a case on an aircraft manufacturer, it should be obvious that entry barriers are high. Despite of this, you could always check with your interviewer about whether your assumption is indeed correct, by saying, "I believe entry barriers are substantial, correct?" Your interviewer would likely not mind confirming this.

It might also always happen that in your interviewer's reply, the answer to a question you were going to ask later on is already included. Make sure you then also capture this information, and leave that particular question out later. For this reason, it is important to understand why each question you ask is relevant, which also explains why you should never go through the list of questions mechanically.

Without a doubt, the business-situation framework will put you on the right track to gain deeper insight into the business case. During the analysis, it is advised that every time you finish a pillar and found relevant information, you make a small interim conclusion. Once you have a good understanding of the business situation, you should aggregate all your findings. Most business cases will however still require you to advance the framework, but in general the business-situation framework will have already brought you quite far. To advance the framework, you use the information collected from the analysis, and further build on the most important insights.

43

The Merger-and-Acquisition Framework

The merger-and-acquisition framework is explicitly designed to analyze merger-and-acquisition (M&A) business cases. Typically, organizations decide to acquire another company and merge with it to sustain their growth objectives or to enter in new markets. When firms eventually decide to acquire another firm, they go through distinctive sequential stages of evaluating different targets, deciding upon an appropriate bidding price and possibly in time merging together. Each stage of the M&A process is quite different and consequently requires a unique analysis. The M&A framework, therefore, consists of discrete components. The first component is used to analyze the fit between a client and potential acquisition targets. The second component is specifically for business cases, where you are asked to determine an appropriate acquisition price, and is commonly used in financial business cases. The last component of the framework evaluates the integration process between merging firms.

In a typical business case, you will almost never be asked to analyze the entire merger-and-acquisition process, but you will rather be required to examine one or two stages of it. Each of these three components are discussed in the following. Keep in mind that each individual component is thus part of the larger M&A process.

Component 1 – Target-fit assessment

The first stage in the M&A process is assessing which potential acquisition targets would match with the corporate strategy of the client. The first component of the M&A framework is specifically designed to structure this assessment, and is essentially a variation of the business-situation framework.

The idea behind the target-fit assessment is to go through the questions of a simplified version of the business-situation framework for both the client and the target companies. The next step is then to assess whether combining the client company with one of the potential target companies looks appealing, taking the objectives of the acquisition into consideration. If, for example, the client wants to enter a specific new growth market, you should look for target companies that are present in that fast growing market. Once you identified the most interesting targets, you need to go more profoundly through the business-situation framework and further investigate the fit between the client and these target companies. If, for instance, a client has great marketing competencies with an unattractive product, and the target company has an attractive product but rather weak marketing skills, then the combined firm would likely be a much stronger firm. This target-fit assessment is structured as follows:

	Customer	Product	Company	Competitors
Client	Main customers?	Main products?	Core competencies?	Main competitors?
Target	Main customers?	Main products?	Core competencies?	Main competitors?
Combined Firm	Which customers would they be serving together?	What would be their combined product offer?	What would be their combined core competencies?	Who would be their combined competitors?

Exhibit 6 - The target-fit assessment framework

In case you have identified a particularly interesting acquisition target, your interviewer may require you to do a valuation or may ask you which problems might occur along the potential merger-integration process. Keep in mind that if the target company has a very similar core business, it is often interesting to combine this assessment with the value-chain framework, and analyze how effectively both value chains could merge and what the benefits of this would be.

Component 2 – Valuation

You will not often be required to do an actual valuation of a target company during a consulting interview, though some business cases do incorporate it. It does happen, on the other hand, that as part of the business case, you are asked to explain how a valuation could be made and which data you would need for this. For this reason, understanding what drives the value of a firm and how you can determine an appropriate valuation for an acquisition target is important.

The most important drivers for a firm's value are considered to be the future cash flows, the discount rate, its growth prospects, and the potential synergies. There are several ways to do a valuation, with the most commonly used valuation techniques being multiples and the discounted cash flow (DCF) method. Both valuation techniques are explained in the following. To obtain a good valuation during your business case, it is always key to have accurate data inputs for the valuation model. Whether you could be provided with sufficient qualitative data inputs generally depends on the size of the target company. Finding accurate data to make an adequate valuation for smaller companies can sometimes be very difficult, whereas it is generally easier for larger corporations.

Multiples, such as the price/earnings ratio, are typically used to get an idea of a possible range for a valuation. The idea is thus to determine an approximate value of a firm by comparing the financial ratios of similar firms. The DCF method, on the other hand, is used to get a relatively accurate idea for a valuation of the target company. The idea behind this method is to look at the expected discounted cash flows over time to determine the value of a business. Notice that the DCF method is based on the NPV, which is explained in chapter 6.

You could still go one step further and decide how much a firm is worth to the client, by including the potential synergies to the valuation obtained with the DCF method. When you then add up both the value of the synergies and the discounted cash flows, you can get a good idea of what a firm is worth to the client. The valuation formula is then in fact a summation of three separate parts, which are the discounted present value (short-term cash flows), the discounted terminal value (long-term cash flows), and the discounted value of the synergies. In the following each of these three parts are briefly explained, together with the formula to calculate them and the key drivers behind these values.

	FORMULA	EXPLANATION	KEY DRIVERS
Present Value (PV)	$PV = \sum_{t=0}^{N} \dfrac{CF_t}{(1+i)^t}$	The discounted value of the forecasted short-term cash flows	• Target attractiveness • Market attractiveness
Terminal value (TV)	$TV_t = \dfrac{CF_t(1+G)}{i-g}$	The discounted future cash flows in perpetuity, using a growth rate 'g'	• Target attractiveness • Market attractiveness
Discounted Synergies (DS)	$DS = \sum_{t=0}^{N} \dfrac{Synergies_t}{(1+i)^t}$	The probability that the synergies can be realized multiplied by the value of the synergies	• Value chain of client & competitor • Business model of client & competitor

Exhibit 7 - The target-valuation framework

where CF_t is the cash flow in year t, $Synergies_t$ refers to the sum of the synergies in year t, i is the interest discount rate and reflects the cost of tying up capital and g is the growth rate, which is assumed constant. For a more detailed explanation on realizing a valuation, we refer to the academic literature on valuation and investments.

By combining all three parts, you obtain a final valuation for the target company. This valuation is often graphically represented as follows:

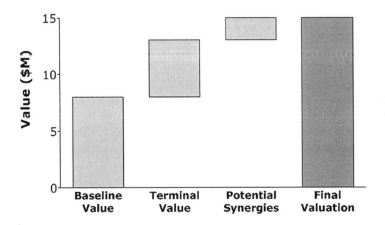

Exhibit 8 - Graphical representation of the target-valuation framework

Keep in mind that the final valuation is often different from the initial bid that a firm makes. This is because the bidding process is normally a negotiation process in which both the client and the target company negotiate the actual acquisition price. It is for this reason that firms often lower their bidding price relative to the obtained valuation. However, when multiple firms are bidding on one target company, the bidding process is often organized through different rounds. If a firm's initial bid is too low, it might be excluded from the next bidding round. The potential synergies and the expected growth rate are usually the most important negotiating points between buyers and sellers. Keep also in mind that these potential synergies are not necessarily the same for the different prospective acquirers.

Component 3 – Merger-integration planning

The third and last component of the M&A framework evaluates the merger-integration process. In reality many companies fail to merge effectively, as it is usually an extremely complex process. The most common reason why mergers are in fact not always successful is because management often does not completely understand the full potential economic value of the acquisition. The merger-integration process often consequentially receives a lower priority and is delayed, resulting in significant economic losses. To avoid merger-integration problems, it is thus critical that everyone in the newly to-be-formed organization understands the full potential of the merger.

The first step, prior to assessing the progress of the merger-integration process, is asking your interviewer whether specific "merger-integration planning" has already been done so far. If this is the case, it is obviously important to understand what has already been realized. The next steps are then to ensure that people understand their roles in the merger-integration process, to ensure that the merger is supported throughout the merging companies, and to investigate the strategic motivations behind the merger. To analyze this, you go through the different pillars described in the framework below, and assess which actions have and have not yet been taken to increase the chances for a successful merger. Given the information received, you should then focus your efforts on those measures that the merging companies have not taken, and explain intuitively how these actions could benefit to the success of the merger and practically be implemented.

STRATEGIC MOTIVATIONS	MERGER TEAM	ORGANIZATIONAL SUPPORT
Ensure the management understands how the merger enhances the company's core strategy. Tailor the integration actions to the specific nature of the merger (scope deal or scale deal?), and integrate where it matters. Make sure the management keeps its focus on the core businesses during the merger-integration process.	Form the project team, and carefully select the leaders of the merger-integration team. Select enthusiastic and talented people with vision, that can further contribute to the success of the merger. Divide all the tasks, resources and responsibilities for the merger-integration process.	Communicate and execute clearly the merger-integration plan, and immediately get the necessary support of both merging companies Create a decision-driven organization in favor of the integration process. Commit to one culture (for example, through compensation programs that reward the behavior you want to encourage).

Exhibit 9 - The merger-integration planning framework

The Value Chain Framework

The concept of the value chain, first described by Michael Porter in 1985, quickly made its way to the forefront as a powerful strategy framework. It has proved particularly helpful in business cases on cost reductions, overall business performance improvement, corporate strategy, and sustaining a competitive advantage. The value chain framework is based on a company's value chain, and specifies how to effectively analyze each element of the value chain. The framework can, in essence, be used for almost all types of companies, and allows a very sequential and logic analysis.

The idea behind the value chain concept is that a product or a service passes through a company's chain of activities, also referred to as the value chain, and at each activity, the product should gain added value. The objective is to maximize in each stage the added value, which should ideally be higher than the costs occurring in that stage. The costs, for example, of adding certain preservatives to a yogurt recipe to avoid it from rotting are low, but the added value on the other hand is rather high. It is important to understand that one value chain activity often affects the cost or performance of the next ones, because they are never isolated from each other. For this reason, it is necessary to optimize not only all the activities individually along the value chain, but definitely also their interrelationships. This way, a firm can align its value chain with its corporate objective and pursue a competitive advantage. This competitive advantage is generally in terms of a cost leadership strategy or a differentiation strategy. A cost leadership strategy has as objective to become the lowest cost manufacturer through a cost-effective value chain. A differentiation strategy, on the other hand, aims to differentiate the product or service through unique features built-in along the value chain, and charge premium prices for these. The value chain is represented as follows:

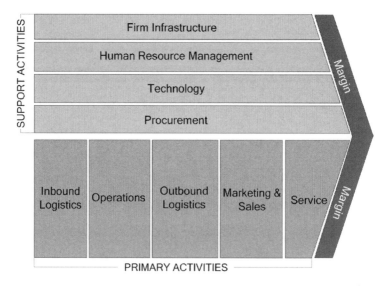

Exhibit 10 - The value chain concept

Notice that there are two types of activities in the value chain: primary activities, which are directly related to the creation and delivery of a product or service, and support activities, which are indirectly related to the product or service and are, in some firms, partially outsourced.

As mentioned before, the value chain framework is fundamentally based on the value chain concept and specifies how to effectively analyze each element of the value chain. The idea behind the framework is to identify which activities in the value chain can be further improved. From there, you can then come up with actionable recommendations that could lead to cost reductions, differentiation opportunities, or to overall business performance improvements. This consequentially increases the total added value, and thus the possible margin that a company has on the products or services it is selling.

The value chain framework will be discussed in detail in the following. The most effective way to work yourself through the framework is by first focusing your analysis on the primary activities of the value chain and, only then start by better understanding the support activities. It is also for this reason that the framework has been split into these two parts. If applicable, you could make an interim conclusion once you have finished one part of the framework. As you will notice, the idea behind the standard questions of the value chain framework is to, first, better understand the particular activity of the value chain and then to analyze and understand its cost per unit, as well as its performance and added value over time relative to competitors or best-practice firms. Keep in mind that these standard questions are sufficient to get a basic understanding of each element in the framework. As always however, you might want to add additional questions to the framework depending on the specifics of your business case.

PRIMARY ACTIVITIES				
Inbound Logistics	**Operations**	**Outbound Logistics**	**Marketing & Sales**	**Services**
How does the inbound logistics system work, and how does it work at the firm's competitors?	How does the operational process work, and how does it work at the firm's competitors?	How does the outbound transportation system work, and how does it work at the firm's competitors?	Which marketing tools and sales channels are used within the firm, and which ones do the competitors use?	Which after-purchase services are provided, and which ones do competitors provide?
How have the inbound transportation costs, material handling costs and material storage costs per unit evolved over time relative to the competitors?	How has the need of raw materials for the operational processes evolved? How have the process costs, handling costs and machine maintenance costs per unit evolved over time relative to the competitors?	How have the outbound transportation costs per unit evolved over time relative to the competitors?	How cost-effective are the firm's marketing tools and sales channels relative to those of the competitors'?	How have the costs per unit of these services evolved relative to the competitors?

SUPPORT ACTIVITIES			
Procurement	**Technology Development**	**HR Management**	**Organizational Infrastructure**
How does the procurement division operate, and how efficient is it in securing the lowest possible price with the highest possible quality for the inputs/raw materials? How have the costs of the purchased inputs, such as raw materials, equipment, and other supplies, evolved over time? Which and how many suppliers are there for the input materials?	Which technologies exist to support the value-creating activities, and what are its costs relative to the competitors? Is the technology infrastructure well streamlined, and does it lower the complexity of the chain of activities?	How does the HR division operate, and does it function in line with the corporate objectives? Are incentives aligned with the corporate strategy? And are there performance measures installed to follow up and reward good behavior? Are the right people working at the right place throughout the organization?	Is the organizational infrastructure, i.e., the company culture, the organizational hierarchy, and the control systems, aligned with the corporate objectives? Is the firm's organization made to sustain and build the value creation along the chain of activities?

Exhibit 11 - The value chain framework

When you eventually have a good understanding of the business case through the value chain framework, you can aggregate all your findings and present them to your interviewer. Keep in mind that in general, you will thus still be asked to advance the framework. To do this, you again use the collected insights from the analysis and build on the most important findings to drive toward actionable recommendations.

BUSINESS CASE EXAMPLES

All the business case examples below are illustrated as actual discussions with an interviewer. This way makes it easier to understand how you would use specific frameworks during an actual case interview. The examples follow the standard approach to business cases, and are categorized by the type of framework used. Some business case examples skip some steps relative to the standard approach to crack business cases, but they all follow the main idea. The examples are written to be as straightforward as possible; it is, however, the logic behind the approach and the structure of the framework that are the reasons why the examples are so easy to follow. Keep in mind that business cases are almost always different, and you should thus never assume that you already know upfront how to crack it. An interviewer can easily make up his or her own variation, and likely will. Therefore, use the examples provided as a study object and guideline, but do not learn them by heart. Last, notice that within the business case examples, brackets were used to specify certain actions to take.

Profit-Problem Framework

Example one:

Interviewer: Our client BicycleCo is a bicycle manufacturer and has seen its profits decrease with 10 percent over the last year. Could you please assess this situation?

You: Before I start the analysis, I would first want to know whether the profit decrease is an industry wide phenomenon, or a particular problem of our client?

Interviewer: Well, the overall industry has seen a small increase in pro-fits. I would say the problem is more client related. Why are you asking?

You: I was interested whether we are dealing with an internal client problem or moreover an external, industry-wide, problem. Can I please have some time to think about a framework for analysis?

Interviewer: That seems a good idea. Let me know when you are ready to start.

You: [Decide on the framework and make a sketch] I decided to analyze the profit decrease by assessing both revenues and costs, using the following framework. [Briefly demonstrate the framework to the interviewer.]

Interviewer: That seems fine. Let us start the analysis.

You: First of all, does BicycleCo sell one or multiple products?

Interviewer: They only sell the BX-5, which is a sports bike.

You: Well, my hypothesis is that the costs stayed relatively constant, and that there has been a decrease in revenues. Let us investigate whether this is correct. As you know, revenue equals sales volume multiplied by the price per unit. Has there maybe been a decrease in sales volume or in the unit price per bicycle?

Interviewer: Actually the price per unit went up with almost 1 percent this year, without an impact on the sales volume. So actually revenues went somewhat up. It has to be said that, generally, the bicycle price is extremely sensitive to larger price changes.

You: Well, my initial assumption seems to be off. Let us then have a look at the cost side of the framework. With how much percent has the total cost gone up relative to last year?

Interviewer: Well, the total cost has actually gone up with more than 10 percent since last year.

You: That is interesting. Let us further investigate this. Has there then been a change in the total fixed cost or in the total variable cost?

Interviewer: The total fixed cost remained relatively stable. I can tell you however that the total variable cost has gone up, because of an increase in the variable cost per unit.

You: Let us then focus on the variable cost per unit (advance the framework). Would it be possible to get a breakdown of all the variable costs per unit of last year relative to this year?

Interviewer: I do not have that information available. But what do you think are the main variable costs per unit?

You: Well, let us see. I would imagine raw materials to be the major variable cost per unit, but also labor costs, marketing costs, handling costs, as well as sales, general and administrative expenses (SG&A) are probably important variable costs per unit.

Interviewer: Those are indeed the most important ones. It actually appears that the raw material costs have gone up enormously, because the price of the metal bike frame almost doubled. What would you suggest our client to do?

You: Well, I would recommend our client to first search for other manufacturers of metal frames with a lower price, that provide a similar quality. If possible, it would also be interesting to investigate where our client's competitors acquire their metal frames, given that they had a small increase in profits.

Interviewer: That seems a good initial recommendation. Thank you very much.

Example two:

Interviewer: Our client BeerCo, a small premium beer manufacturer in Australia, has seen its profits decrease with almost 10 percent relative to the same period last year. Could you assess the situation, and explain what has happened?

You: Before starting, I have a question. Is the recent profit decrease an industry-wide phenomenon, or an issue at our client?

Interviewer: The premium beer industry has seen a small drop in profits over the last three months relative to the same period last year, but then we are talking about 1 or 2 percent maximum.

You: Right, so the overall industry seems to only explain a minor part of the recent drop in profits.

Interviewer: It appears so.

You: Ok, please allow me some time to think about how I would structure this problem.

Interviewer: Ok.

You: [Decide upon the framework, and draw it out.] I decided to analyze the profit decrease by having a look at both revenues and costs, using the following framework. [Briefly explain the profit-problem framework to the interviewer.]

Interviewer: That seems a good approach to better understand the problem.

You: First of all, I would like to know whether our client sells one or various premium beers?

Interviewer: BeerCo only sells one premium beer.

You: OK. Let us first have a look at the cost side of the model. Has there maybe been an increase in the costs recently? And if yes, is this cost increase related to the total variable costs or the total fixed costs?

Interviewer: There has indeed been a cost increase. The cost of one specific raw material has namely increased, resulting in an increase in the variable cost per unit of roughly 2 percent. This raw material is an atypical ingredient, specific to only BeerCo's premium beer.

You: In that case, only BeerCo is affected by the cost increase, and thus not its main competitors. On the other hand, this still does not fully explain the drop in profits of 10 percent. Let us now have a look at the revenue side of the model. Revenues equal the sales volume multiplied by the sales price. Has there been a change in the sales price or perhaps in the total sales volume?

Interviewer: The sales price did not change; the sales volume however strongly decreased over the last two months.

You: Interesting, the major driver behind the fall in profits then seems to be the decrease in sales volume. This together with the small drop in industry profits, and the price increase of one of the raw materials seems to explain what has happened.

Interviewer: That looks correct. Could you maybe further analyze why the sales volume has decreased?

You: [Advance the framework.] Maybe it would be interesting to have a look at the customers, the product, the client, and the main competitors [the business-situation framework]. We already have a fair amount of information on the client, and we also know that the competitors have seen a small decrease in profits. Therefore, I suggest we first have a look at the customers and the product. I first want to better understand our client's product. Could you tell me something more about the product itself?

Interviewer: Well, as I said, it is a premium beer sold at a premium price. The product's quality is of high standard, and the customers tend to be very sensitive about that. It should also be said that BeerCo's customers are not that price-sensitive.

You: Has there maybe recently been a change in product packaging, in product ingredients or in the product recipe?

Interviewer: The packaging did not change, but four months ago, our client had to change to another supplier for hops, which is a key ingredient to make beer. The reason is that its supplier went bankrupt, though the new supplier has the same variable cost per unit.

You: This could possibly explain the decrease in sales volume. How long does it take for the product to go from the production line to the store?

Interviewer: It takes roughly two months, meaning two months of stock more or less. Why?

You: Well, since the premium beer with the new hops are for sale in the stores, which is thus since two months, sales have been going down. One possible explanation is that the new hops supplier does not provide the same quality as the previous one. Did BeerCo collect any customer data since it has received product from this new supplier?

Interviewer: Well, actually the new supplier was the only one offering the same price per ton as the previous supplier. Our client did recently organize a blind tasting to collect customer information. The data indicates that customers are less excited about the beer that contains the new supplier's hops.

You: The fact that the new hops are less appreciated by BeerCo's customers, together with the fact that customers are very quality-sensitive, seems a reasonable explanation why the sales volume has dropped.

Interviewer: That seems a good explanation. What would you suggest doing about this?

You: Well, as you mentioned BeerCo's customers are very quality-sensitive, but not that price-sensitive. Therefore, I would recommend our client to switch to a hops supplier that provides the same or a higher quality than its previous supplier and possibly charge the difference to the customer. This seems for me the way to go; however, some further research would have to be done to identify the most interesting supplier.

Interviewer: That is a good suggestion.

Business-Situation Framework Example

Interviewer: One of our key clients AirplaneCo, an aircraft manufacturer in North America, has seen a small decrease in its share price over the last four months. What is worrying our client, however, is that their main competitor, PlaneCo, has seen an increase in its share price in the same period. Could you assess what is going on, and come up with some recommendations?

You: To better understand the context of the case, I would first like to have an idea of the size of our client and the types of airplanes it produces.

Interviewer: For the first question, I am not sure about our client's total revenues, but last year's net profit was about US $3 billion. Almost all of the airplanes sold are commercial airlines.

You: OK. Now I have a better idea of what kind of client we are dealing with. Could I have a minute to structure my thoughts and decide how I would like to analyze this case?

Interviewer: Sure. Let me know when you are ready.

You: [Decide on the framework and draw it out.] I decided to analyze this situation by having a closer look at the customers, the product, our client, and the competitive environment. [Briefly demonstrate the framework to the interviewer.] By asking targeted questions about each of these, I think I should be able to get a better understanding of what has been going on. If you agree with this approach, I feel that I could start with assessing our client, unless you already have an idea where the problem might be situated?

Interviewer: I think your framework should be fine. Could you first, however, start with analyzing the competitive environment?

You: Of course. Could you tell me then how the industry is structured? Also, I would like to know whether you have any information on the relative market shares of our client and its competitors, and how their market shares have evolved?

Interviewer: Well, in North America there are two main players in the passenger aircraft industry. Our client has about 50 percent of the market share, and their main competitor PlaneCo has about 40 percent of the total market share; the other 10 percent is divided among three smaller players. These market shares have been relatively stable over the last years in terms of revenues.

You: Interesting. Given the share price increase, it seems PlaneCo has been performing well according to the market. Do you have any information on whether PlaneCo recently changed its strategy? Additionally, I would like to know on what basis competition generally takes place.

Interviewer: PlaneCo did not change its strategy recently. I would almost say business has been as usual for them. For your second question, I would say competition is mainly focused on quality, though price is also an important factor.

You: Just to be sure, is there any new industry regulation I need to be aware off?

Interviewer: The aircraft manufacturers industry is highly regulated, but this is not important for this case.

You: It seems to me that the problem might not be competition related. Let us now have a closer look at our client.

Interviewer: Ok.

You: Given that our client competes in the aircraft manufacturing industry, what are its specific core competencies? And, furthermore, is it involved in particular adjacencies?

Interviewer: Generally AircraftCo's main strength is to deliver quality-aircrafts on-time through flawless project management, and its customers have always praised this competency. To answer your second question; our client focuses all its efforts on its core business and is not involved in any specific adjacencies.

You: OK. How have revenues and costs evolved over time relative to PlaneCo?

Interviewer: Well, revenues are mostly driven by the company's order book, which shows the total number of airplanes ordered. Because of this, current revenues are driven by payments of earlier-made orders. Both AircraftCo and PlaneCo have received numerous orders in the previous years. I can tell you that both companies have had stable levels of revenues and costs over the past three years.

You: That is interesting. How about nowadays, did AircraftCo and PlaneCo receive a lot of new orders in their order book?

Interviewer: Well, PlaneCo saw a moderate increase in orders relative to the last years, but AircraftCo saw a small decrease relative to the previous years. Some customers even recently cancelled their order of Aircraft-Co's newest model and ordered aircrafts from PlaneCo instead.

You: This seems very valuable information, and I will definitely come back to it later. [It thus seems that the main problem is situated with AircraftCo's newest airplane model.] Let me further assess the situation. Did our client make any major investments recently? Or did it encounter any operational issues?

Interviewer: It did not make any recent major investments. It did, however, encounter some operational issues because of a strike at the supplier for the cockpits. Because of this, the delivery of three airplanes has been delayed.

You: This late delivery, and the small decrease in orders of AircraftCo's newest model, might explain the stock price decrease. Let us now have a closer look at the customer.

Interviewer: Ok.

You: Who are the customers, and are there specific customer segments? Also, are the customers concentrated or dispersed, and are we meeting their needs?

Interviewer: Our client's customers are mainly the airline companies, and they could be segmented, but that is not necessary for this case. They are quite concentrated, although the number of aircraft producers is even smaller. The customers have generally been satisfied with the quality of the aircrafts, though recently they have been more skeptical.

You: That is interesting. Let us then have a look at the product. Why have clients recently been skeptical about the quality of the aircrafts?

Interviewer: Well, recently two of our customers have experienced technical issues with AircraftCo's newest airplane model, which has been in the news. There seemed to have been a serious problem with the airplane engines, which are made by an external supplier, and both airplanes needed to make an emergency landing.

You: That probably explains why some customers recently cancelled their order.

Interviewer: Yes. That is indeed correct. It seems we are running out of time. Could you please summarize your findings?

You: The stock price of our client most likely declined because of two main reasons. First, previously sold airplanes of the newest model have had serious technical difficulties, and the bad publicity resulted in a loss of orders. Eventually customers ordered the planes at PlaneCo, which could also justify partially the increase of their stock price. Last, there has been a strike at a supplier of our client, leading to a delay in delivery. Given that our client is respected for on-time deliveries, this might have had an impact on its reputation and also, on its stock price.

Interviewer: That seems correct. Do you have any immediate recommendations for our client?

You: Well, to be sure, I would have to do some further analysis, but it seems our client might be too depending on the supplier for cockpits. Furthermore, AircraftCo should immediately set up a project team with the engine supplier for the newest airplane model to address the technical issue with the engines. If this problem would continue to occurr, it would obviously have a serious impact on the amount ordered, and thus on the bottom line.

Interviewer: Thank you for your recommendations.

Merger-and-Acquisition Framework Example

Interviewer: Our client CandleCo, a candle manufacturer, has recently taken over LightCo, another company specialized in manufacturing candles. The CEO of CandleCo recently explained to me that the merger-integration process has been quite difficult, and he requested our help to effectively merge the firms. Could you assess the reason behind the merger-integration problems, and come up with practical recommendations?

You: Before starting my analysis, I have one specific question. Have specific efforts to merge the companies already been made?

Interviewer: Well, the management has currently set up several dedicated project teams to deal with the merger. These teams have, however, not been successful.

You: Interesting. Let me think about how to structure this problem [Given this specific business case, it should be clear that you will need the merger-integration planning framework. Draw it out, and explain it briefly to your interviewer]. I believe we need to further investigate the strategic motivations behind the merger. We also need to make sure that people understand their roles in the merger-integration process and ensure that the merger is supported throughout the merging companies.

Interviewer: That seems a good idea.

You: Well, let us then first have a look at the strategic motivations behind the merger. What is the primary reason behind the merger, and how is it supposed to enhance the core strategy?

Interviewer: The main reason the management of CandleCo decided to take over LightCo is to remain competitive in the luxury soap market. Several important cost reductions will need to be realized to achieve this objective. Combined they have a market share of about 30 percent, but the market is dominated by LuxCandle who controls about 55 percent of the luxury soap market. The entire management is well aware of the strategic importance of the merger.

You: Given that both firms were competing in the exact same market, it seems to me that the deal was thus part of a scale deal?

Interviewer: That is correct. An immediate scale increase was indeed needed to remain competitive relative to LuxCandle. Both the management of CandleCo and LightCo realized this in time.

You: Have they already determined where in the value chain the potential scale benefits are situated, and how these will be realized?

Interviewer: The management already calculated the potential savings because of the scale increase, and created project teams to efficiently realize these savings.

You: Has the top management been able to keep its primary focus on maintaining the core business, or did it somewhat lose focus of its core business because of the ongoing merger-integration process?

Interviewer: The top management has kept its primary focus on sustaining the core businesses, and has carefully been following up the market share and the competitive responses to the merger.

You: It appears thus that the management is well aware of the strategic importance of the merger, and that they, in the mean time, have been able to keep their focus on the core business. Let us now have a look at the operational efforts that have been taken so far. As you mentioned, the management did set up project teams to effectively merge both companies. Did they also decide who would be leading these merger-integration project teams, and allocate the resources and responsibilities? Did they furthermore choose enthusiastic and talented people to build the newly to-be-formed organization?

Interviewer: Well, as said, the project teams have been set up by the senior management. All the roles and responsibilities related to the merger-integration planning are quite straightforward. The project teams are, however, not working efficiently. The management had difficulties finding people that are enthusiastic about the merger, since most people in the organization appear to be nervous about it.

You: That is interesting. Let us have a look at how the merger is supported throughout the organization, and come back to this later. Did the management clearly communicate the merger-integration plan and the strategic motivations behind it to ensure that all employees understand their role in the newly formed organization?

Interviewer: The management communicated the merger-integration plan immediately, and did several efforts to win the hearts and minds of all the people involved. Nonetheless, many employees still seem to be nervous about the merger. What do you think can be the reason that several people are so nervous about the merger? [The interviewer wanted you to answer this and, therefore, comes back to it immediately.]

You: Well, given that the merger involves important cost reductions, I presume that certain job positions might have become uncertain?

Interviewer: That is indeed correct. Some jobs will be cut, but most importantly, it seems that many previously promised loan increases cannot be guaranteed anymore. Several employees are nervous and less motivated because of this. There, however, seems to be another important problem that is troubling the success of the merger-integration planning.

You: Ok. Did the management point out the key areas of focus to make the merger-integration a success? Did it set up a decision-driven organization that focuses its efforts on the critical decisions to make the merger succeed?

Interviewer: The management is trying to create a decision-driven organization, and clearly communicated on which areas the project teams should focus their efforts. Even though many employees in the organization are nervous about the merger, it appears that they are perfectly aware of the priorities related to the merger-integration planning. They have, on the other hand, been extremely ineffective in executing the tasks in practice.

You: Interesting. What were the previous corporate cultures of both CandleCo and LightCo like? Furthermore, did the management do any specific efforts to commit to one culture, consistent with the new strategy behind the merger?

Interviewer: Well, CandleCo has always been known to be a very innovative and dynamic company. LightCo, on the other hand, is known to be a rather conservative company. The management only did some minor efforts to commit to one 'new' culture.

You: It appears that both corporate cultures are extremely different, which is likely leading to ineffective decision making and poor task execution.

Interviewer: That is indeed correct. Given your analysis, which practical course of action would you suggest the management takes to blow new life in the merger-integration plan and get the maximum support along the organization?

You: The management should clearly communicate how the merger will exactly affect the employees. Furthermore, the management should emphasis the importance of working together as one team, to ensure that the potential job losses and the pressure on the promised loan increases do not get worse. In addition, the management should commit to creating one culture, based upon the new strategy behind the merger. They could realize this by setting up compensation programs that reward the behavior they want to encourage, or maybe by creating successful team-building events.

Interviewer: Thank you very much for your analysis. Merger-integrations are often very complex, and as you noticed, many things can go wrong.

Value Chain Framework Example

Notice that this example briefly starts with the internal profit-problem framework, and eventually switches to the value chain framework to progress in the analysis and crack the business case.

Interviewer: Our client ExpressCo, a package-delivery services company operating in Australia, has seen its overall profit margin shrink over the last two years. Could you analyze the situation and come up with actionable recommendations to improve ExpressCo's overall profit margin?

You: Of course. I first, however, have two questions. First of all, would you say that the profit margin decrease is an industry trend or an issue specific to ExpressCo? Second, would it be possible to already briefly explain to me how the industry is structured in terms of major players and market shares?

Interviewer: The package delivery market in Australia exists of three players, namely, ExpressCo, TransportCo, and DeliveryCo. Each company has a market share equal to about one-third of the total market. I would say that the overall profit margin decrease is rather unique to ExpressCo, given that its competitors have had a relatively stable overall profit margin, which is currently higher than the profit margin of ExpressCo.

You: Interesting. [You could use the internal profit-problem framework to start the analysis] I suggest we then first have a look at the revenues and costs to better understand what is driving the decreasing overall profit margin. [Draw out the framework.] Did the overall profit margin decrease because the costs have gone up faster than the revenues, or because revenues have fallen more relative to the costs? In addition, I wonder how the revenues and costs individually have evolved relative to those of TransportCo and DeliveryCo?

Interviewer: ExpressCo has seen an increase in both its revenues and costs. TransportCo, DeliveryCo and ExpressCo have identical revenues and fixed costs. ExpressCo however currently has a much higher total variable cost relative to its competitors.

You: It appears thus that the total variable costs are the reason behind the profit margin decrease relative to the competitors. The total variable cost equals the number of 'produced services' multiplied by the variable cost per unit. I assume that the customers of package-delivery companies in general immediately pay for the package-delivery service and, thus, that the sales volume will be very similar to the number of delivered services. I therefore assume that the problem will be on the variable cost-per-unit side?

Interviewer: That is correct.

You: Well, before further analyzing the variable cost per unit, I would like to know which types of delivery services ExpressCo and its competitors provide?

Interviewer: All three companies provide very similar delivery options. There is the standard delivery, the express delivery, the premium delivery, and the enterprise delivery. They all have very different variable costs per unit.

You: How did the variable cost per unit evolve for all these delivery options relative to DeliveryCo and TransportCo?

Interviewer: I would say that the standard delivery, the express delivery, and the premium delivery have always had very similar variable costs per unit and sales volume for all three companies. ExpressCo's variable cost per unit of its enterprise delivery package is, however, much higher than the variable cost per unit of the enterprise delivery package of its competitors. ExpressCo decided to internalize this extra variable cost per unit that it has relative to its competitors. All three companies are charging the exact same price for the enterprise delivery service. ExpressCo is consequently making less profit on this package relative to its competitors. Additionally, all three firms require their customers to pay an extra fee, based upon the distance from the distribution center to the final delivery address.

You: It appears thus that the lower profit margin on the enterprise delivery package is driving the decreasing overall profit margin relative to TransportCo and DeliveryCo. Are there any important differences in how ExpressCo processes the enterprise delivery packages relative to its competitors?

Interviewer: There are indeed some differences in the way ExpressCo handles their enterprise packages relative to its competitors. Nonetheless, the total revenue and the revenue growth for the enterprise packages is about the same for all three companies.

You: It then appears that ExpressCo's enterprise delivery package has a much higher variable cost per unit relative to its competitors because they construct this service differently. Customers, however, apparently do not particularly value ExpressCo's enterprise delivery service more, given that its revenue and revenue growth have been similar to those of its competitors. I think it would be interesting to have a look at ExpressCo's value chain and assess how the enterprise packages are handled throughout the value chain, and analyze what drives the higher variable cost per unit relative to DeliveryCo and TransportCo. [Move from the internal profit-problem framework to the value chain framework, plus draw out and briefly explain this new framework.]

Interviewer: That seems like a good idea.

You: To start, I would first like to know how the inbound logistics system to collect the enterprise packages works for all three firms. Furthermore, I am wondering how the inbound transportation costs, package handling costs, and package storage costs per unit for the enterprise packages have evolved over time relative to both competitors.

Interviewer: All three firms directly pick up the enterprise packages with specialized vehicles at the customer, which are generally large companies. They then transport the collected packages to the closest distribution center to store them. About 90 percent of their customers are situated in Sydney, Melbourne, Brisbane, Perth, or Adelaide, and they all have a distribution center in these cities. The inbound transportation costs, the package handling costs, and the package storage costs per unit are essentially the same for all three firms.

You: Is there a difference in how all three companies process the enterprise packages internally? Furthermore, does ExpressCo have higher process costs, handling costs, or system maintenance costs per unit relative to TransportCo or DeliveryCo?

Interviewer: All companies have a specific division that processes the enterprise packages, because the process is quite different to that of the other delivery packages. To process the enterprise packages, ExpressCo actually uses an older, almost outdated, technology than its competitors. Because of this, ExpressCo has a higher cost per unit to process and handle the packages, and the system maintenance costs are higher for ExpressCo relative to its competitors. This however still does not entirely explain the lower profit margin for the enterprise packages.

You: Interesting. Let us now have a look at the outbound transportation system. How has the outbound transportation cost per unit evolved over time relative to the competitors?

Interviewer: ExpressCo actually has a much higher outbound transportation cost per unit than its competitors. What do you think drives the outbound transportation cost per unit?

You: I imagine that it is mainly driven by the distance from the customer to the nearest distribution center, the price of gas, the wages of the driver and the average gas consumption per mile of the vehicle to transport the enterprise packages.

Interviewer: Those are indeed the most important drivers of the outbound transportation cost per unit. Which parameter do you think, explains the difference in the outbound transportation cost per unit?

You: I assume that the wages of the vehicle drivers are quite similar across the industry, and furthermore, I assume that the average paid gas price for all three firms is probably similar. The gas consumption per mile of the vehicles might be different, because the competitors might have a more energy-efficient vehicle fleet. Furthermore, it is actually possible that they fill up their vehicles with more enterprise packages per trip, leading to fewer rides and thus generally a lower average outbound transportation cost. Last, it could be that the final delivery addresses for ExpressCo are on average further away from the distribution center than for its competitors.

Interviewer: Your assumptions are correct. All three companies furthermore have on average about the same load of enterprise packages per trip. Also the average distance from the distribution center to the final delivery address is quite similar for all three companies. Actually, this could indeed have a negative impact on the outbound transportation cost per unit. It would however not necessarily have a negative impact on the profit margin, given the distance-based fee. TransportCo and DeliveryCo have, on the other hand, bought new, energy-efficient vehicles over the last two years, specifically for the delivery of the enterprise packages.

You: That is interesting. With the increasing gas prices, it seems sensible that both DeliveryCo and TransportCo have been able to keep a significantly lower outbound transportation cost per unit thanks to their new energy-efficient delivery vehicles, which has not been the case for ExpressCo.

Interviewer: That is correct. This however still does not entirely explain the lower profit margin for the enterprise package-delivery service.

You: Let us then have a look at the marketing and sales costs per unit for the enterprise package. Which specific marketing tools does ExpressCo use, and how cost-effective are they relative to both competitors? Furthermore, which are the primary sales channels used by ExpressCo, and which ones are used by its competitors?

Interviewer: All three companies solely use their company website to sell the enterprise package delivery service. Customers simply fill in where the package needs to be picked up and where it has to be delivered, and then they process the payment. All three companies have a relatively small sales cost per unit. The marketing cost per unit for the enterprise package is however much higher for ExpressCo than for its competitors. All three companies nonetheless use the same marketing channels to promote the enterprise package delivery service, namely newspaper advertisements, direct mail, and targeted online advertisements.

You: ExpressCo's higher marketing cost per unit then further explains why the profit margin of its enterprise package delivery service is lower relative to DeliveryCo and TransportCo. Since ExpressCo does not have a higher revenue or revenue growth rate relative to its competitors, it seems to me then that ExpressCo's marketing campaigns are less efficient than those of its competitors. Could you tell me what the share of usage is of these marketing channels for all three companies?

Interviewer: I have no specific data on that available. I however do know that TransportCo and DeliveryCo have started to make more use of targeted online advertisements relative to ExpressCo. ExpressCo on the other hand uses much more newspaper advertisements relative to its competitors. Online advertisements are actually far less costly than newspaper advertisements, but are equally effective in targeting interesting enterprise package delivery customers.

You: It seems to me then that ExpressCo could lower its marketing cost per unit, while maintaining its total revenue and revenue growth, by making more use of targeted online advertisements, and investing less in newspaper advertisements.

Interviewer: That is definitely correct.

You: Let us now have a look at the after-purchase services that go with the enterprise delivery package. Which after-purchase services do ExpressCo and its competitors provide? And, second, how have the variable costs per unit of these services evolved relative to both competitors?

Interviewer: All three companies provide the exact same after-purchase services, and these all have a similar variable cost per unit.

You: Interesting. So far I have found out that the lower overall profit margin is driven by the relatively low profit margin of the enterprise delivery packages. Right now, I see three main reasons for this. First of all, ExpressCo has a higher variable cost per unit to process and handle the packages, because it still uses an older technology for handling the enterprise packages. Also the system maintenance costs per unit are higher because of this. Second, ExpressCo has less energy-efficient vehicles relative to its competitors for delivering the enterprise packages. Therefore the outbound transportation cost per unit is higher for ExpressCo. Lastly, ExpressCo makes much less use of the more cost-efficient targeted online advertisements relative to its competitors. Therefore, ExpressCo has a higher marketing cost per unit for similar marketing campaign results. We could now additionally analyze the support activities, such as procurement or HR management, which are indirectly related to the delivery service.

Interviewer: I believe you already have identified the most important drivers behind the lower overall profit margin. For the support activities, I could tell you that ExpressCo's procurement department has a good reputation. Also the HR management and the firm infrastructure operate perfectly in line with the corporate objectives of ExpressCo. As you already identified, ExpressCo is somewhat behind with its technological infrastructure, and will need to replace and streamline its technology to lower the variable cost per unit of the enterprise delivery package. Could you now come up with actionable recommendations to improve ExpressCo's profit margin?

You: Given the identified problems, I would recommend the management of ExpressCo to invest in a more modern technology to process the enterprise delivery packages. Furthermore, I would recommend them to invest in more energy-efficient vehicles for the delivery of the enterprise packages. Last, I recommend ExpressCo to make more use of targeted online advertisements, given that they are much more cost-efficient. To make the investments, ExpressCo will, however, first need an adequate amount of cash. Therefore, it would be interesting to investigate the capital requirements to practically implement these recommendations and, in case ExpressCo would not have sufficient cash reserves, also how it could raise this capital.

Interviewer: Thank you very much for your analysis and recommendations.

WHAT IF IT DOESN'T FIT?

It is definitely possible that you would come across a business case that does not really seem to fit any of the standard frameworks. This, however, does not mean that the case cannot be structured. When this happens, strive to find out what precisely is driving the problem through 'segmentation'. You start by isolating the problem and focus on finding the actual reasons why the numbers are so low or high. Break the issue down into its components by segmenting it in different ways, and determine what contributes to the majority of the problem. Once identified, it is a matter of using common sense to figure out how you can address these specific issues.

For example, you might have a business case concerning a manufacturer of mobile phones that has a high production error rate relative to its competitors, and he wants to know the reason behind this. You could then use the value-chain analysis and focus on the questions appropriate to analyze problems in manufacturing processes. It might however be smarter to immediately start segmenting along various parameters that could drive the difference in the error rate. You might, for instance, segment the error rates per product type, per production plant, and per specific production process. This segmentation might tell you that all types of mobile phones have about the same percentage of errors and that there are no significant differences in error rates between different production plants, but that 90 percent of the errors occur in one specific phase of the production process. Now that you have identified the major problem driver, you can further analyze how that particular process works and use common sense to come up with practical solutions to solve the issue.

HOW TO MAKE YOUR OWN BUSINESS CASES

Once you fully understand the approach to business cases and have studied the frameworks and their corresponding examples, it is time to create your own business cases and practice them. You can make business cases for yourself, but eventually, the most effective way to prepare is by making business cases in a group and practicing them in pairs. It might initially take some time to create your own business cases, but you will notice that you get better over time.

To make your own business case, the easiest methodology is to first decide on a framework you would like the interviewee to use. Then you draw it out, and decide where in that framework you will 'introduce' some business issues. You then decide upon an industry where these issues could occur, and research the specifics of that industry. You could additionally make a data table or a chart to make the business case more realistic. Finally, as an interviewer, think about which questions the interviewee might ask during the interview, and reflect on how you would reply to them. Keep in mind that you should guide the interviewee throughout the case, but make sure that he or she eventually can come up with the important insights of your case.

10 BEST TIPS FOR BUSINESS CASE SUCCESS

1. Listen to your interviewer. When your interviewer presents the problem, make sure you understand it completely, as well as what is expected from you. Often interviewees make the mistake of answering the wrong question. Furthermore, many interviewees are so focused on asking the right questions that they forget to actually listen to the answers they receive. Therefore, always pay attention to your interviewer, respond to the obtained information, and use it in your analysis. Notice that by carefully listening to your interviewer, you might additionally obtain some interesting hints and insights regarding how to solve the case.

2. Ask questions. One of the worst mistakes made by interviewees is asking their interviewer too few questions. Keep in mind that you need to ask enough relevant questions in order to understand and solve your business case. Make sure that at any point in time, you understand the business case you are dealing with. If some issues are unclear, just ask your interviewer for further information to fully understand the case. Also make sure it is clear to your interviewer why you are asking these questions and why you need that specific information. Do not make direct assumptions, but first ask your interviewer whether he or she has specific data available.

3. Set out a structure. After the interviewer introduced the business case, take the time to think out a structure to organize and analyze the case. Use a framework, and if needed, make some adaptations relative to the specific content of the case. Furthermore, think about the sub-questions that you need to answer first, in order to address the overall issue. Remember to stay structured and organized during the entire process. If your interviewer wants to go in another direction, for instance, by introducing a new document, understand the impact it has on your proposed structure and adapt accordingly.

4. Think aloud. Demonstrate your thought process to the interviewer, as well as how you structure things and come to conclusions. If you have considered some alternatives and rejected them, then tell your interviewer what you did and why. This is eventually the only way your interviewer can assess your performance. If you are not completely comfortable with reasoning aloud, you should practice this by yourself until you become more comfortable at it.

5. Lay out a road map for your interviewer. Next to having and following a clearly defined structure, you should always communicate it to your interviewer. Use your proposed structure as a road map for the interviewer. By doing this, your interviewer can better follow what you are currently analyzing, and what you still have to do.

6. Take notes. Make sure you have a pen, a pad of paper, and a marker readily available to use during the business case. In general, you are always allowed to take notes, and you should definitely do this. From the moment your interviewer presents the case, take notes and try to capture all relevant information. You could use your pen and paper to make little diagrams or figures to demonstrate your reasoning to the interviewer. Furthermore, use the marker to highlight important information or conclusions so you can easily find them again. You should thus use these tools to organize your own thinking, as well as to demonstrate your reasoning process to your interviewer.

7. Summarize. Briefly write down all your conclusions during the business case and, as said, preferably highlight them with a marker. At any time, your interviewer could ask you to summarize and conclude your findings. When summarizing, you should generally start with your main conclusion for the case, and then provide the two or three best arguments to support this conclusion. In case you did not finish the business case in time, present your actual findings in a logical way, focusing on what you did find.

8. Practice a lot upfront. Make sure that you have practiced and have prepared each phase of the case interview sufficiently, and especially that you have practiced enough business cases upfront. Notice that having a clear understanding of how consulting interviews exactly work will give you a significant advantage over other candidates.

9. Don't be afraid of numbers. Many candidates start panicking from the moment they have to make a mathematical calculation during the business case. Make yourself comfortable with basic arithmetic formulas, as well as working with large numbers. Keep in mind that, generally, these calculations are relatively straightforward, and they should never be a reason to start panicking.

10. Be enthusiastic, relax, and enjoy. It is very important to be enthusiastic throughout the interview. Interviewing someone who is excited to be there is much more enjoyable for the interviewer, than someone who does not seem to care about the interview. Furthermore, try to be as relaxed as possible, and enjoy the business case. After all, the business case is to some extent a reflection of what you would be doing on the job.

Chapter IV

Presentation Cases

INTRODUCTION TO PRESENTATION CASES

While traditional case interviews are by far the most common method to screen potential candidates, it seems that many consulting firms are now incorporating another interview technique. This interview technique is the presentation case, where candidates are asked to present and discuss a specific topic to one or more interviewers. Generally, you will be given a stack of documents that form a business case, which you have to summarize and eventually present within a predefined timeframe. Sometimes firms might ask candidates to complete an unfinished presentation, and provide the key insights. Last, some firms will even ask you to prepare a presentation at home, which you then have to give during the interview. Presentation cases are usually part of a second round interview, and will rarely be an integrative part of a first interview round.

The reason why many consulting firms are incorporating presentation cases in their interview rounds is because the case interview is in a number of ways also an imperfect evaluation tool. A traditional case interview will for instance give the interviewer only little insight into the interviewee's presentation skills and his or her client skills. The presentation case on the other hand allows the interviewer to profoundly assess your presentation skills, and get an idea of how you would interact with clients. In general presentation cases are designed to evaluate the following skills:

- **Aggregating a set of data:** Generally, you will be given a large set of data and information, which you will need to process quickly on your own to come to a conclusion. Its main difference with a traditional business case is that for presentation cases, you will have to analyze and combine the facts and eventually wrap up your findings without any guidance.

- **Case-cracking skills:** Just like in a traditional case, your problem-solving skills to structure your insights will be tested. Where in a traditional business case your interviewer will generally confirm the framework you use, here you will be responsible yourself to find the right methodology to crack the case. Most presentation cases, however, already provide clear insights into what the output should look like.

- **Presentation skills:** Obviously, during a presentation case, your presentation skills will be assessed. Keep in mind that whatever level you enter a consulting firm, you will always have to present your findings to your case team or client, and this is thus a very important consulting skill. By far the most important for a good presentation, is the way you structure your findings to make them easy to understand. The most common way to structure presentations logically is the "top-down" approach, in which you start very broadly and zoom in on the major issues or opportunities.

- **Your teaching skills:** On the job, you will often have to formally or informally debrief your team or your client. Therefore, during a presentation case, the ability to teach content and explain the reasoning behind your analysis will be evaluated. Obviously, during a traditional case interview, the interviewer could get some insight into your teaching ability, but the presentation case allows the interviewer to go much further and to understand how well you can communicate and transfer your ideas to someone else.

- **Team skills:** Presentation cases were often used in the context of a group discussion with several candidates together. This allowed the interviewer to also assess your team skills, which could work to your benefit, especially if you are particularly good at building team consensus. Nowadays, however, many firms are starting to use the presentation case on a more individual level.

All these skills will be very important on the job, and many consulting firms are trying to incorporate the presentation case at some point in the interview cycle. The reason presentation cases are still not very common, is because organizing them is often quite time-consuming, and thus expensive, for consulting firms.

Below you will find a methodology, which will allow you to structure most presentation cases. Keep in mind that some consulting firms might indicate to you what the output should look like. Keep in mind that if the presentation case does not seem to fit the proposed methodology below, you should not try to squeeze it in. The proposed structure will however help you to organize the majority of presentation cases.

STRUCTURING YOUR PRESENTATION CASES

In general to solve a presentation case four key steps can be identified:

1. Clarifying and understanding the question
2. Skimming the materials
3. Building the framework and cracking the case
4. Structuring the presentation logically

In the following, each step is explained in more detail. The focus is mainly on step four, as it is the most challenging part of a presentation case. Remember that it is important to set a timeframe from the start on how long you will work approximately on each step. The type of presentation case will generally determine how much time you will have to spend on each step. Very quantitative cases often for instance require some extra time to crack the numbers; very qualitative cases however often require some more time to go through the text materials. It is only by practicing case presentations in advance, for instance by making up presentation cases yourself, that you will become better at estimating your time needs.

1. Clarifying and understanding the question

The first thing you want to know when you start a presentation case is what you are expected to do in terms of final output. It is often a good idea to ask the person that gave you the presentation case whether you could go through the questions together, to ensure you are clear on the expected output. This to make sure that once you are on your own, you are clear about which questions you should be answering. In case you would be told that the questions are clearly explained in the exercise, you can obviously assume they are, since generally the questions you will need to answer are included in the package of information that you are given for the presentation case. Make sure that you read the questions several times, to ensure that you are completely focused on what you are expected to deliver and that there is no ambiguity in what your final output should look like.

Furthermore, you also need to know at this stage who your audience will be. Often a presentation case is given within a specific context, and the person or people you will be presenting to will be playing a specific role. In a presentation case on a post-merger-integration plan, you might, for instance, be presenting to two consultants "playing" the role of the two CEOs of the two companies that would be merging. Obviously, knowing who your audience is will help you to better understand what your final output should look like. The presentation of a post-merger-integration plan you would give to the two CEOs would for instance be quite different from the one you would give to the two CFOs. Clearly a CEO is more interested in the overall challenges and opportunities of the integration plan, whereas a CFO is in first instance more interested in the costs and benefits of this plan. Therefore, always ask which role your audience will be playing. Notice, however, that for quite a few presentation cases, the role of the audience can be less important or even irrelevant. But if the interviewers do "play" specific roles, be sure to know which ones.

2. Skimming the materials

In the second stage, it is time to start reading the materials. Some presentation cases have a very limited set of documents, and if time allows, you may be able to read each document in detail. Most often, however, presentation cases are accompanied by a large amount of information. The trick is then to be able to skim through all the information efficiently by focusing most of your attention on reading the titles, subtitles, specific text, figures, and graphs and by making sure you get the main idea of each document. Notice that these documents could be one or multiple pages. It is advisable to number each separate document from the start, and when you start skimming through all the documents, write on a separate sheet for each document in one line what the key message is. Your final output should then be a list of numbers with each time a key message next to it, for each specific document. Collecting and aggregating this information will allow you to eventually get the bigger picture. It is then recommended to select the two or three most important sources from which you will be taking most of the information. When you have done all this, you will know what each document's key message is, and you will better understand the bigger picture. In case you feel that you are still missing some information, you could start reading some documents in more detail. Nonetheless, always make sure you are keeping track of time, as you should allow sufficient time for the next two steps.

3. Building the framework and cracking the case

The approach you take to construct the framework and to solve a presentation case is generally the same as for a traditional business case. Therefore, for this section, please refer to the previous chapter on how to crack business cases.

The only difference with a presentation case is that you will not have your interviewer to check whether you are following the right approach.

Nonetheless, you can first skim through all the documents before deciding which framework would be the most suitable, whereas with a traditional business case, you have to make a decision relatively quickly about how you will structure the business case. Start by asking yourself which framework would best fit the presentation case, given the information you acquired while skimming the documents. If, by using the framework you have in mind, you are capable of structuring most of the important elements of the case, then it is likely to be a good choice.

4. Structuring the presentation logically

The structure you use for your presentation obviously depends on the information you are given, as well as the questions you are supposed to answer. For smaller presentation cases you might be asked to only briefly present your findings on one slide. For longer presentation cases, however, you are generally expected to present your findings in a very structured manner using multiple slides, or several pages on a flipchart. For this reason a framework has been created, which allows you to organize most longer presentation cases. Keep in mind that for some presentation cases, a more customized structure might be necessary to logically present your findings.

The framework to structure presentation cases consists of the following five elements:

a. Introduction
b. Executive summary
c. Situational overview
d. Response plan
e. Next steps

The following discusses which information of your analysis you should include in each of the five elements of the framework. It is often a good idea to name each slide according to these five sections, unless you have a better, more specific, title in mind. Doing this will allow your audience to easily know what you are about to present.

a. Introduction

The first thing you might want to do when you have to present the presentation case is "frame the case," which means putting the case in a more realistic context. A good way to do this, is by welcoming the audience and saying what you have been analyzing. This introduction should only take about ten to twenty seconds, but should immediately demonstrate that you have a professional approach to the case.

Depending on the case, an example of an opening line could for instance be "Thank you to the board for making time today to discuss the cost reduction plan for the soap manufacturing plant in Houston. I have collected and analyzed significant information, and would like to present a summary of my key findings, and discuss where we can go from here."

Most other books covering presentation cases will typically advise you to immediately start with an executive summary. If you would however start framing your presentation with your executive summary on the background, your audience will immediately start reading that, instead of listening to your introduction. Therefore, it is recommended that you first start with a very simple slide that for instance gives the name of the company you have been analyzing and the type of analysis you have been doing, for example, "Analysis of the cost reduction plan." Doing so will guarantee that you have your audience's attention. Keep in mind that in this stage, you are only framing your presentation, and thus not yet giving any information on the actual case. After you have framed the presentation case, you can immediately move on to the executive summary.

b. Executive summary

The executive summary is one of the most important parts of a presentation, as it is meant to deliver the key messages of the case. Unfortunately, many interviewees presenting a case forget to include an executive summary. They instead start presenting their detailed analysis right away, and thus skip this critical step. The idea of an executive summary is to make your audience quickly acquainted with what you are about to explain them later in detail. Your slide with the executive summary should contain your two to three most important insights derived from your analysis. The idea here is not to start explaining how you came to these insights, but to already give an update to your audience. In case someone would already ask how you came to these conclusions, it is perfectly fine to say that your analysis will be explained further on in the presentation. Remember that how you actually came to your key insights, should eventually always be explained further on in your presentation.

c. Situational overview

In this part of the presentation, you give a structured overview of the current situation, and address all the key issues and/or opportunities.

It is here where you will apply your framework, and discuss all the dimensions important to understand the current situation. If one aspect of your framework is more important than the rest, discuss the less relevant dimensions only briefly and state that your analysis focused particularly on a certain part of the framework. Once you have provided the overall situational overview through your framework, you start focusing on where the issues and/or opportunities are situated (i.e. advancing the framework).

Make sure you present the situational overview in a logical way, for example, by starting very high-level (such as the total market or the entire corporate value chain) and gradually move down, to identify and discuss the issues or opportunities at a more detailed level (for instance, sales opportunities in the Canadian market or relatively high costs-per-unit in the sales department).

Last, it is advised, where relevant, to use visuals to explain your ideas. Remember that a picture is worth a thousand words. This can go from simple symbols, such as arrows or boxes to more advanced charts. When you are given a set of quantitative data, you should consider how you can best present this in your presentation to describe the situation and support your insights.

d. Response plan

In some presentation cases, you will be asked to only analyze the current situation, by identifying the current issues or opportunities. Often, however, you will be expected to go further and determine potential responses to address the current situation. In other words, you then need to determine the consequences of your analysis. If you, in the previous step, for example, identified that a client's sales department is cost inefficient compared to its competitors, you should now identify potential measures to reduce this cost and, if possible, quantify the potential monetary savings of these actions. Depending on the context of the case, your analysis and recommendations might, on one hand be quite abstract, or might on the other hand be descriptive and precise.

One good way to present your response plan is by ranking the possible actions from highest priority to lowest priority. First, present the key implications of your analysis, and leave the smaller implications for discussion at the end. Keep in mind that your actions should be realistic. If for instance your conclusion is to shut down a small manufacturing plant, at least discuss the potential difficulties of this measure, such as strikes in other plants or additional costs due to severance pay. Last, when you present the key consequences of your analysis, a good way to close is by asking the audience if they would like to discuss or consider any other actions.

e. Next steps

Not all presentation cases require you to discuss the next steps, but including it shows you are not afraid to think further than the case requires. The idea is to briefly discuss what should be done after this presentation, generally in terms of additional analysis or even practical implications. The objective here is not to be very accurate about what should be done next, but rather to make some suggestions about which additional pieces of analysis would be interesting to further progress in the case. Avoid making a large list of potential next steps, but rather, try to identify the two analyses that would have the highest value for future progress in the case.

Examples of such "next steps" could, for instance, be further analyzing the potential cost savings, quantifying in detail the sales opportunities in the Canadian market, or creating an implementation plan for the suggested measures from the response plan.

A last slide you could always include, is a slide that says "Questions & Answers" or simply "Q&A." This makes it clear that your presentation is over, and that you are ready to address the remaining questions your audience might have. Most interviewers will however already have asked most, if not all, their questions during the presentation. Nonetheless, some interviewers tend to keep a number of questions for you to answer at the end.

TIPS FOR PRESENTATION CASES

These are the three most important tips for success on presentation cases:

• **Make sure you have fully understood the assignment from the start.** This cannot be emphasized enough. Generally you will be on your own when preparing the presentation, and thus you have to ensure that there is no ambiguity on what your output should look like.

• **Keep an eye on the time!** Having done an extensive analysis, but eventually not having anything on the slides, demonstrates you are not able to manage your time effectively or even that you were too slow with processing the information. Therefore it is critical to decide from the start how much time you will spend on each phase of the process to solve the presentation case, and try to stick as much as possible to this time schedule.

• **Be ready for questions.** Rarely will your audience just listen to you without any interaction. Make sure you always know the reasoning behind what you are saying, as you could always be asked about it. If you are asked about a certain number or a piece of data, and you are not sure, never make something up. Instead, you should go back to the data and make sure you provide a correct answer. In case your audience asks a question that you will address later on, you should tell them that you will address that particular issue later on in your presentation.

Chapter V

Guesstimates and Brainteasers

WHAT ARE GUESSTIMATES?

The guesstimate question, or guesstimate, is a special type of question that you can expect to be asked during a consulting interview. The idea is that you are asked to make an educated guess at something for which you normally do not know the answer, and for which you have to logically derive a realistic estimate. An example of a guesstimate could be: "How many family cars are bought each year in the United States of America?" Guesstimates are specifically designed to assess your strengths in the following areas:

- **Logic:** Are you able to come up with a structured approach to find an answer?
- **Numerical skills:** Are you comfortable with making fast calculations with large numbers?
- **Creativity:** Can you find multiple ways to derive an answer or a backdoor to a quicker but accurate answer?
- **Professionalism:** Are you able to remain calm when being confronted with a complicated guesstimate?

Guesstimates are typically asked during the first interview round, and only occasionally in later rounds. Make yourself comfortable with the structure to solve guesstimate problems through continuous training, and you will notice significant improvements in your skills to solve this type of problem.

Always keep in mind that for a guesstimate question, it is better to arrive at a moderately wrong answer using a structured methodology with good assumptions, than to immediately give the correct answer because you read it last week in the newspaper. Giving the right answer without making a logical analysis will not impress your interviewer, as this is not the goal of a guesstimate. On the other hand, you could impress your interviewer by indicating multiple strategies to come to a good estimation.

Often, guesstimates are given as in-case guesstimates, in which the guesstimate is part of a larger business case. For example, in a business case on a solar panel manufacturer in France, the interviewer could stop you before starting the business case, or even in the middle of your analysis, to ask you an estimation of the total solar panel market in France. Sometimes the interviewer will expect you to use your estimation in the business case; sometimes, the interviewer will ask you to go back to the business case without actually using the estimation. Another possibility is that you get a guesstimate and a business case unrelated to each other, often in a first interview round. In some consulting firms, you might get one or two stand-alone guesstimates in the first round and no business cases until the second round.

Every guesstimate is different, and most guesstimates can be solved in multiple ways, using different methodologies. Nonetheless, there are some good strategies that will help you to solve most guesstimates. The most common strategy is the "top-down" approach, in which you start broadly and then slowly drill down to find the answer. The strategy is demonstrated in the guesstimate examples section. This approach will help you solve most guesstimates; nonetheless, some guesstimates demand a more customized approach in order to be solved.

Generally, when solving guesstimates, it is important that you first understand what is required. For instance when you are supposed to estimate how many taxis are operating in New York, you should obviously understand that you eventually need to come up with a certain number of cars. When starting your analysis, it is also important to understand whether your interviewer will provide you with specific information or whether you will have to make assumptions. You can determine this by checking your first assumptions with the interviewer. In case he or she refuses to comment on your assumptions or indicates that he or she does not know, then you will have to assume the answer yourself. If the interviewer does provide you with data, make sure you use this to come to your final answer.

After you are given a guesstimate question, feel free to take a moment to think over the best approach to solve it. You could, for instance, say, "What an interesting question; please allow me some time to think about how I will approach this." Use this time effectively to consider an approach, such as for example the top-down approach. If possible, try to go for a methodology with which you do not have to make complicated or highly uncertain assumptions. When you eventually come to an answer, never forget to do a reality check by simply verifying whether your answer seems realistic. If your calculation, for instance, shows that in the United States, every day, 1 million serious car accidents happen, you clearly made a wrong assumption or used an incorrect methodology. In case you realize that you, in your approach, went wrong somehow and your outcome is unrealistic, make sure to indicate to your interviewer that you are aware of this. Then investigate what might have gone wrong, such as an incorrect assumption or a miscalculation, and redo the estimation from the point where you went wrong.

When you arrive at a good estimate, you might be able to "triangulate" your answer. Often it is namely possible to approach a guesstimate using different methodologies. You could work out an estimation using one or two different approaches and compare or even average the outcomes. This demonstrates to your interviewer open-mindedness, as you recognize more than one way to solve a problem. Keep in mind, however, that time is scarce at a case interview. Therefore, you could simply suggest, after having made your first estimation, alternative approaches without actually working them out. Note that your interviewer might ask you at the end of the exercise whether your answer seems realistic to you. This, however, does not necessarily mean your estimation is wrong; it just means your interviewer wants you to do a reality check. In case your answer seems realistic, you could simply state that your outcome does seem realistic to you. Your interviewer might simply want to see whether you will stand your ground or whether you start to have doubts about your approach. In case the estimate does not seem sensible, be honest and have a look at the assumptions and methodology you used, and try to correct where relevant. Keep in mind that if you use good assumptions and a correct methodology, then your interviewer will always appreciate your efforts, even when your estimation is slightly off compared to the actual answer.

It is important to mention that, generally, when solving guesstimates you will be calculating with large numbers. If you have not practiced this for a while, it is definitely advisable to practice your mathematical reasoning skills beforehand. Some interviewers even allow you to use a calculator; thus, make sure you have one at hand. Generally, however, your interviewer will expect you to make the calculations unaided. Keep in mind that you are allowed to round up the numbers you are calculating with. Rounding down the US population to 300 million is generally fine; rounding down the number of days in a year to 300 however, is not. Make sure you do not exaggerate with rounding numbers, though you should not give yourself too much of a hard time calculating with difficult numbers either. Try to strike the right balance between rounding down and deriving a realistic answer.

Last, it is recommended that you in advance study some important numbers by heart. You should for instance know some facts and figures about the country in which you are applying for a consulting position, such as its total population and other general demographics. It would also be smart to have an idea about the usage of Internet, mobile phones, cars, and so on, in your country. Furthermore, you should know the global population, as well as have an idea of the population of some of the world's most important economic countries, such as China or the United States. The more figures you know the better, but keep in mind that your focus is on preparing for case interviews, not studying a series of figures by heart.

GUESSTIMATE EXAMPLES AND SUGGESTED SOLUTIONS

In the following, examples of guesstimates using both the top-down approach as well as more customized approaches are provided. Keep in mind that all the solutions for the guesstimates are based upon assumptions and approximations.

Example one: How many children are currently born each year in the United States?

Answer: The main driver for the number of children born every year in the United States is the total number of fertile woman. Our starting point for this guesstimate would be the total US population, which is 300 million people. Assuming half of this population is female, we have a total of 150 million women. Let us say that most pregnancies occur between the ages of 18 and 38 for women, thus during a span of twenty years. Knowing that the female life expectancy in the United States is about 78 years, about one out of four people (25 percent) would be between 18 and 38 years old when we assume that every age is equally represented. However, younger people are more represented than older people, though not that much anymore in industrialized countries. Let us, therefore, assume that 30 percent of the women are between 18 and 38 years old. This would mean 45 million women in the United States are aged between 18 and 38 years.

Let us now assume that on average women give birth to two children during their fertile period of twenty years. Obviously some women do not want to have children or have only one; others have three children or more. Regardless, this would mean that they have on average two babies over twenty years, or one baby every ten years. Assuming that the number of fertile women remains relatively constant over the next ten years, which is a sensible assumption, then 45 million women will give birth to 45 million babies in a period of ten years. We thus have 45 million babies born in ten years, which means 4.5 million babies born every single year in the United States.

The most recent exact birth figures in the United States show that about 4.3 million babies are born every year, which is clearly quite close to our estimation of 4.5 million births per year. It is very important to understand, however, that as the total US population grows over the years, the assumption of 300 million inhabitants also changes, and thus the estimated number of childbirths.

In order to impress you interviewer even more, you might want to add that you could find a slightly better estimate when for instance taking into account infertility rates for women and men. Several other factors that have an effect on the number of childbirths in the United States can be imagined. Obviously, all these factors have a relatively minor impact, but demonstrating that you can think further shows creativity and open-mindedness to your interviewer, and will only do good for your overall performance.

To summarize:

300 million US citizens; 150 million of those are woman. 45 million (or 30 percent) of those are between 18 and 38 years old. 1/10 chance that these women will give birth in a particular year. Thus, 45 million × (1/10) = **4.5 million childbirths in the United States per year.**

As you can see, the top-down approach, in which you drill down from a broad population to find a reasonable estimation to answer the question, has been used.

Example two: How many marriages currently occur each year in the United States of America?

Answer: Two important drivers behind the total number of marriages every year in the United States of America are the number of marriages a US citizen has on average during his or her life, and obviously the number of US citizens.

Let us assume that on average each US citizen has one marriage during his or her life span. Obviously some people never get married; others have more than one marriage during their lives. Nonetheless, one marriage during a life span seems a reasonable assumption. Furthermore, it seems sensible to assume that most people have their marriage between 18 and 53 years of age, assuming that the number of marriages after the age of 53 or before 18 are nominal. Knowing that the average overall life expectancy in the United States is about 78 years, close to half of the people (45 percent) would be between 18 and 53 years old, if we assume that every age is equally represented. Let us assume that about 50 percent of the people are between eighteen and fifty-three years old, knowing that people in their thirties and forties are represented more than the average. With a total US population of approximately 300 million people, with 50 percent falling into our category, we have 150 million citizens aged between 18 and 53 years old. With one marriage on average within a time period of 35 years, chances of a marriage in a particular year are theoretically about 3 percent. With 150 million candidates, having a 1/35 chance on average to marry in a particular year, we have about 4.3 million US citizens on average who would marry this year. Given that people of course get married in couples, we have to divide this number by two to find our estimation for the number of marriages in the United States. This brings us to a total of 2.15 million marriages every year in the United States. The most recent statistic on the number of marriages in the United States per year shows a total of 2.2 million marriages, which is very close to our estimation of 2.15 million marriages per year.

It would also have been possible to not estimate the number of citizens at a marriageable age in the US, but just say that a person marries once in an average life of 78 years. This would mean 300 million people with a 1/78 chance to marry in a particular year, thus leaving about 3.8 million people to marry on average per year in the United States. This thus means an estimated 1.9 million marriages per year. As you might have noticed, this method skips the estimation of people at marriageable age. On one hand, you have less risk for making an error; on the other hand, you are claiming that one could marry at any age, which is less realistic and, in the end, slightly less accurate.

To summarize:

300 million US citizens; 150 million (or 50%) of those are between eighteen and fifty-three years old. 1/35 chance that these will have their marriage in one particular year, thus 150 million × (1/35) = 4.3 million people on average get married per year in the US; and 4.3 million people who will marry means 4.3M/2 = **2.15 million marriages per year in the USA.**

Or shorter:

300 million US citizens, and 1/78 chance that these will have their marriage in one particular year. Thus 300 million × (1/78) =

3.8 million people on average get married per year in the United States; and 3.8 million people who will marry means 3.8M/2 = **1.9 million marriages per year in the USA.**

Again the top-down approach was used, which drills down from a broad population to find a reasonable estimation to answer the question.

Example three: How many (75cl) standard bottles of wine are consumed in the United States each year?

Answer: The main drivers for this estimation are the number of adults, as well as the popularity of wine in the United States. There is a total population of 300 million people, and let us say that about 75 percent are adults, meaning 225 million people. Let us furthermore assume that about 80 percent of them consume alcohol, meaning 180 million people. Obviously not everyone who drinks alcohol drinks wine. Let us assume that of those people that consume alcohol, about 70 percent would consume wine. This brings us at a total of about 125 million people in the United States who consume wine. Clearly consumption levels vary greatly between different people, but let us say based upon intuition that an average person that drinks wine, realistically consumes three full glasses of wine per week. This implies that each week 375 million glasses of wine are consumed in the United States. Assuming that one standard wine bottle of 75cl would on average serve five glasses of wine, we find a total weekly consumption of 75 million bottles of wine. On a yearly basis this would mean a total consumption of 3,900 million bottles of wine. When we now have a look at the actual number of wine bottles consumed per year, we find a yearly consumption of 3,875 million bottles, which is remarkably close to our estimation.

To summarize:

300 million US citizens, and 225 million of those are at an adult age (75 percent). 180 million of them consume alcohol (80 percent), and 125 million of them consume wine (70 percent). Average wine drinkers consume 60 percent of a standard bottle per week; thus 375 million glasses, or 75 million bottles, of wine are consumed per week. This gives 75 million × 52 weeks = **3,900 million wine bottles (of 75cl) per Year**.

Obviously, there is no need to be this close to the exact number, because making accurate assumptions is about good intuition and insight, but is also still partially luck. If we, for instance, had said the average wine drinker consumes five glasses per week instead of three glasses, the estimation would have been much less accurate (6,500 bottles). Nonetheless, keep in mind that the interviewer expects you to have a strong and correct approach; making a minor assumption error will however be forgiven. Therefore, it is key to initially figure out a proper methodology; one that preferably uses uncomplicated assumptions, to come to an approximation. Whether your final estimation is very accurate or not matters to a lesser extent. Notice again that the top-down approach has been used, which drills down from a broad population to find a reasonable estimation to answer the question.

Example four: How many passenger cars are in use on our planet?

Answer: This guesstimate has been asked during an interview with Arthur D. Little, and is a tricky one. Also this guesstimate can best be solved using the top-down method starting from the global population, which is close to 7 billion people. One difficulty we now have, however, is that the usage of passenger cars over various continents and countries varies considerably, and therefore, it is quite difficult to estimate a global percentage of passenger car owners. You could make an estimate, but there is the chance that you might be far from the correct answer. Instead, you should divide the problem into smaller sub-problems, also referred to as "grouping," and then use the top-down methodology within each "group." In this case, for instance, you could estimate the percentage of car users per continent, leaving out Antarctica obviously, which would mean six groups. You then, however, need to have an idea of the number of inhabitants per continent and make sure the total adds up to 7 billion. Furthermore, you should have a sensible intuition on the percentage of passenger car owners per continent. You would then come up with something similar to exhibit 12.

Estimations:	North America	South America	Europe	Asia	Oceania	Africa
Population	450M	500M	500M	4.25M	50M	1.25M
Car owners	60%	20%	45%	4%	55%	2%
Total passenger cars	270M	100M	225M	170M	28M	25M

Exhibit 12 - Estimated number of passenger cars by continent

Adding all the estimations of passenger cars used per continent, we find 818 million passenger cars in use on our planet. The actual amount is not known, but well-thought-out estimates range from 750 to 950 million passenger cars worldwide. Again, demonstrating a good methodology to your interviewer is more important than coming up with an almost perfect estimation.

Notice that other ways of grouping could be used to come to a realistic estimation. You could, for instance, separate groups by yearly income, including all non-adults in the no-income category, and estimate the number of people per category and the percentage of those that would own a car. This would give something similar to exhibit 13.

Estimations:	High income (>30K annually)	Average income (10K - 30k annually)	No/Low income (<10K annually)
Population	400M	1.1B	5.5B
Car owners	95%	15%	3%
Total passenger cars	380M	165M	165M

Exhibit 13 - Estimated number of passenger cars by yearly income-level

Adding up all the individual estimations, we find a total of 710 million passenger cars worldwide, which again is a good estimation.

This guesstimate may be one of the more difficult ones, given that you need to have quite some pre-knowledge to make adequate groups. Nonetheless, this guesstimate has been asked during an interview, and you should thus be prepared to come up with a good estimation. As mentioned before, make sure you study upfront some figures about your own country, as well as some global figures on population, car ownership Internet usage, and so on, as they might come in very helpful when solving guesstimates.

Example five: How many traffic lights are there in Manhattan?

Answer: Clearly, the number of traffic lights depends mainly on the number of street crossings. Let us assume that in Manhattan every street crossing has on average five traffic lights installed, and let us now approach Manhattan as a rectangle, with 250 blocks along 14 avenues. This means a total estimated number of 3,500 intersections in Manhattan. Taking an extra step, we could subtract Central Park, which covers a total space of about 50 blocks by four avenues, meaning 200 fewer intersections. This brings us to a total estimated number of intersections of 3,300. Given our assumption of five traffic lights per intersection, we find a total estimated number of traffic lights of 16,500. We could now for instance add 10 percent to this number for temporary traffic lights because of construction works, which brings our estimation to about 18,000 traffic lights in Manhattan.

The exact number is evidently unknown, but the goal is only to demonstrate a correct methodology and ßreasonable assumptions. Obviously to effectively answer this question, you need to have an idea of what Manhattan looks like. Therefore, this question would more likely be asked in the United States, and even more likely in the New York office.

To summarize:

Manhattan has 250 blocks and 14 avenues = 3,500 intersections. If we deduct Central Park: 50 blocks by 4 avenues = 200 intersections, we have 3,500 − 200 = 3,300 intersections, with 5 traffic lights on average per intersection. 3,300 × 5 = 16,500 traffic lights + 10 percent for temporary traffic lights, thus 16,500 × 1.1 = **An estimated 18,000 traffic lights in Manhattan.**

Example six: Estimate the total market for toilet paper in the United States

Several guesstimates involve estimating the market for a certain product or service. You should thus be able to do a market estimation of about any product/service, definitely for your own country. Regularly your interviewer will, in this case, use this estimation as a starting point for a business case.

Answer: Again multiple methodologies can be imagined to make this estimation. You could start with the number of US citizens, and then estimate the average toilet paper consumption based on intuition. Another approach would be to start from one average person's yearly toilet paper usage and generalize to the entire US population. This strategy is also known as a "bottom-up" approach, and is used to make the estimatation in this example.

Let us say that the average US citizen uses on average 15 times per week toilet paper, consuming 25 toilet paper sheets each time. With 52 weeks in a year, we find then that 19,500 toilet paper sheets are used every year per person. Given that there are 300 million inhabitants in the United States, we would have a total annual consumption of 5,850 billion toilet paper sheets. Let us say that an average toilet paper brand's 12-pack with 350 sheets per roll retails for $7 (probably $6.99). These packs then contain 4,200 toilet paper sheets, and we would, thus, have an annual consumption of 1.4 billion of these toilet paper packs. With each of those standard 12-packs costing $7, we would estimate that the annual toilet paper spending in the United States is $9.8 billion.

Example seven: Estimate the total yearly revenue of McDonald's in the United States.

Answer: Several approaches can again be imagined. You could, for instance, use the top-down method starting from the total US population, and estimate how much an average inhabitant spends per year at McDonald's. Another good methodology would be to divide the US population in, let's say, four groups: frequent consumers, average consumers, infrequent consumers, and non-consumers. You could then estimate how many people fall in each group and estimate their yearly McDonald's spending to find a good estimation. For this guesstimate, we used the second approach; grouping. First, we start with the total US population, which is about 300 million people. To determine how many people are frequent, average, infrequent, and non-McDonald's consumers and how much people in each category would spend on average in McDonald's, you eventually need to use your intuition. You would then come up with something similar to exhibit 14:

Estimations:	Frequent consumers	Average consumers	Infrequent consumers	Non-consumers
Total people per category	5M	30M	165M	100M
Average Weekly (yearly) Mc-Donald's spending per person	$10 ($520)	$2 ($104)	$0.5 ($26)	$0 ($0)
Yearly Mc-Donald's spending per category	$ 2,600M	$ 3,100M	$ 4,300M	$ 0M

Exhibit 14 - Estimated spending at McDonald's by consumption-level

Adding up all totals, we eventually find a total of 10 billion in annual sales in the United States. McDonald's real sales figure for the United States is close to 8 billion annually, which is relatively close to our estimation.

Example eight: How many tennis balls could you fit in an average-size private swimming pool?

Answer: Before throwing yourself into solving this guesstimate, you might want to ask your interviewer what he or she considers as an average-size private swimming pool. If he or she gives you certain dimensions, you will obviously need to work out the answer using these. Otherwise, you will need to make an assumption on the dimensions of an average private swimming pool.

The best way to solve this guesstimate is to first estimate the volume of an average private swimming pool, and then estimate the volume of a tennis ball. You can then easily calculate the number of tennis balls that would fit in this swimming pool. Assuming that the interviewer did not give any specific swimming pool dimensions, we could estimate an average private swimming pool to be 15 ft by 30 ft (4.6 m x 9.2 m), with an average depth of 5 ft (1.5 m). These dimensions imply a total volume of 2,250 ft³ for our average private swimming pool.

Let us now estimate the volume of one tennis ball. The formula to derive the volume of a ball is $(4/3) \times \pi \times (radius)^3$. Let us assume that the radius of a tennis ball is about 1.2 inches, or 0.1 ft. This gives us a total volume for one tennis ball of $(4/3) \times \pi \times (0.1 \text{ ft})^3 \approx 4 \times (0.001 \text{ ft}^3) = 0.004 \text{ ft}^3$. By dividing the total estimated volume of an average private swimming pool (2,250 ft³) by the total estimated volume of a tennis ball (0.004 ft³), you would find that 562,500 tennis balls would fit in this average-size swimming pool. Nonetheless, the calculation is not yet finished. Taking the extra step, we need to take into account the fact that tennis balls would never stack perfectly on each other, but would moreover "fit" into each other. Because of this effect, the height of the stacked balls would be slightly lower, allowing for, let's say, about 10 percent more tennis balls in our swimming pool. This brings our estimate to about 620,000 tennis balls that would fit in the average-size swimming pool.

Creating Additional Guesstimates

The more you practice guesstimates, the better you will become at it. Therefore, creating some additional guesstimate questions for further practice is recommended. One great way to do this, is to ask a friend to look up some interesting figures on the Internet that you then estimate. Ask him or her to give you the guesstimate questions, make the derivations yourself, and check your estimation afterwards with the exact answer. If you were relatively close to the correct answer, you should move on to the next question. If, however, you were not, you should have a look at your assumptions and methodology to find out where you might have gone wrong.

If you find you still need extra practice to improve your guesstimate skills, you could read *Guesstimation: Solving the World's Problems on the Back of a Cocktail Napkin* by Lawrence Weinstein. This book is devoted to mathematical approximation, and the author discusses several approximation techniques in detail. Additionally, many other books that discuss case interviews have a section on guesstimates.

WHAT ARE BRAINTEASERS?

Brainteasers are complex riddles that, in order to be solved, require some serious thought. They are designed to test your logic skills and creativity, which are important attributes for a consultant. Brainteasers are however far less common in case interviews than are guesstimates, but nonetheless, you might be asked to solve one.

Keep in mind that there is no specific type of brainteaser, as they come in many forms, and the best approach to tackle them often differs. For some brainteasers, you will need your mathematical insights to reach an answer, while others will instead require some out-of-the-box thinking. Because brainteasers are generally quite unstructured, it is evidently difficult to suggest a full-proof step-by-step methodology to solve them. Nonetheless, you can significantly improve your skills to solve brainteaser by practicing multiple examples. It is advised that when you are given a brainteaser, you immediately write down the specifics of the brainteaser and make sure you have understood the problem correctly. One common strategy that often helps to solve a brainteaser is to initially simplify the problem to gain insights, and then generalize your simplification to solve it. This strategy is demonstrated in the example section. Lastly, keep in mind that some brainteasers have several possible solutions, with some even being quite obvious.

Even though most consulting companies discourage the use of brainteasers during interviews, every year some interviewees receive a brainteaser in their first or second round. As brainteasers are generally not part of a standard interview, only a small number of fully worked-out examples are illustrated.

BRAINTEASER EXAMPLES AND SUGGESTED SOLUTIONS

In the following, some examples of brainteasers have been provided. As you will notice, the level of difficulty will increase with each example.

Example one: A man wakes up early in a hotel with no working lights and must dress for work. He puts on his outfit, but when he gets to his socks, he realizes that he has twenty different socks in his suitcase: ten white and ten black ones. How many socks does he need to take to assure himself that he will have at least one matching pair?

This brainteaser is relatively easy and has been asked in a first round interview at Roland Berger Strategy Consultants.

Answer: The first thing you could ask your interviewer is whether it would make sense to open the curtains to let the sun come in. The interviewer would appreciate your creativity, but normally he would answer that it is still too dark outside.

Let us first simplify this problem by looking at what the man should do if he had only two different pairs, one black and one white. This makes the guesstimate look somewhat easier and allows you to better imagine the situation. Now, first, you should try to imagine yourself being in this position. You would first pick one sock out of four, which could be black or white, you don't know. When you now take a second sock, this could again be black or white. One possibility is that it is the same color as the first sock; in this case, you have a matching pair already. The other possibility is that it is not the same color as the first sock; in this case, you would have already taken one black and one white sock. If you then take one more sock you would definitely have one matching pair, whatever color this third sock is. It will thus take the man at most three attempts to have a matching pair of socks.

Obviously, the reasoning and the eventual answer for ten white and ten black socks is exactly the same, but the problem might seem to be more complex. By simplifying the number from ten to two pairs of socks, it however becomes easier to get a better grip on the brainteaser.

Example two: You are given two empty buckets, one capable of holding 3-gallons and the other 5-gallons. How could you use these two buckets to fill a 4-gallon bucket? You have a water tap available that you can use to fill the 3-gallon and the 5-gallon buckets.

This brainteaser is also rather easy, and comes from the movie 'Die Hard: With a Vengeance'. Two strategies can be used to arrive at a correct answer.

Answer: The best way to solve this problem is by trying out different possibilities until you find one that works. It might help if you sketch the buckets, to better visualize the situation.

One possible solution would be to first fill the 5-gallon bucket, and empty it into the 3-gallon bucket, which leaves 2 gallons in the 5-gallon bucket. Now empty the 3-gallon bucket, and pour the 2 gallons in the 3-gallon bucket. Now fill the 5-gallon bucket, and use it to fill the 3-gallon bucket. Once the 3-gallon bucket is full, you will be left with 4 gallons in the 5-gallon bucket.

Another possible solution would be to first fill the 3-gallon bucket and pour it all into the 5-gallon bucket. If you then fill the 3-gallon bucket again, and use this to completely fill the 5-gallon bucket, you would be left with one gallon in the 3-gallon bucket. Now, empty the 5-gallon bucket and pour 1 gallon in this 5-gallon bucket. When you now fill the 3-gallon bucket and pour this in the 5-gallon bucket (which already has 1 gallon in it), you will eventually have 4 gallons in the 5-gallon bucket.

Example three: You are faced with two doors. Behind one is a pot of gold; behind the other one is nothing. In front of each door is a person; one always lies, and the other one is always honest. You can only ask one question to one person to decide behind which door the pot of gold is. Which question will you ask in order to get the pot of gold?

This brainteaser is already more challenging than the previous two. Two questions could be asked to find out which door is the correct one.

Answer: First, it might be useful for you to quickly sketch the situation. Obviously you cannot just ask a person behind which door the pot of gold is, as there is the possibility that you asked the person that always lies. The idea is to find a question to which both doorkeepers would indicate the same door. You can achieve this by making the liar take the perspective of the honest person and vice versa. Both ways to do this will now be illustrated.

One possible solution would be to ask to either person, "If I would ask the other person which door would lead to the pot of gold, what would he answer?" In case you would have asked the liar, he would indicate the wrong door. The reason is that he knows that the other (honest) person would indicate the right door, and so he lies about this. In case you would have asked the honest person this question, he would also indicate the wrong door, as he knows the other (lying) person would indicate the wrong door, and he is honest about this. With this question, both people will indicate the wrong door, and you can thus conclude you should take the other door.

Another possible solution would be to ask, "If I would ask the other person which door does not lead to the pot of gold, what would he answer?" In this case, the reasoning is similar, but both people will indicate you the correct door, where you should go to find the pot of gold.

Example four: Five pirates have captured one hundred gold coins and should divide them among themselves. The most senior pirate has to propose a distribution for the coins. If at least 50 percent accept his proposal, the coins are divided as proposed. Otherwise, he will be executed and it starts all over, and the new most senior pirate will have to make a new proposal. What division should the most senior pirate propose, assuming they are all rational and greedy?

This brainteaser is definitely challenging and requires some more thought.

Answer: For this brainteaser, it would definitely be a good idea to again simplify the question, and gradually make it more difficult before reaching the correct answer. In this case we could analyze what would happen in case there would be one, two, three or four pirates instead of immediately five. Let us in the following say that pirate one is the least senior and pirate five is the most senior.

We will first have a look at the problem if there would only be one pirate. In that case, he would simply take everything for himself. If there were two pirates, than pirate 2 would propose to allocate all coins to himself. By voting on himself, he would have fifty percent of the votes and thus obtain all coins. Let us now analyze what would happen in case there were three pirates. In this case the most senior pirate would need at least one other pirate to accept his proposal; if not, he gets executed. Pirate 3 should realize here that if he were executed due to his own proposal, there would only be two pirates left, and as we just figured out, pirate 2 would then get all the coins, leaving no coins for pirate 1. Therefore, if pirate 3 would propose to give one coin to pirate 1 and ninety-nine for himself, then pirate 1 would definitely agree. This is because pirate 1 knows that if he does not accept this proposal, pirate 3 would be executed and pirate 2 would eventually assign all the coins to himself. Let us now analyze what would happen if there were four pirates. Pirate 4, the most senior one, would then have to convince one other pirate in order to obtain the minimum of fifty percent acceptance. Again, he knows that if he were executed, that pirate 3 would keep ninety-nine coins for himself, and give one to pirate 1. Pirate 4 could, in this case, convince pirate 1 by giving him two coins, and pirate 1 would accept, as two coins are better than one. Pirate 4, however, has an even better option: he should propose to give one coin to pirate 2, and ninety-nine for himself. Pirate 2 will accept this proposal, as he realizes that in case pirate 4 would get executed he would get nothing from pirate 3. If we now look at the original situation where there are five pirates, then pirate 5 would need two other pirates to vote for him. The two pirates he will need to convince are those that get nothing in the scenario where pirate 4 decides. Therefore, the solution for pirate 5 would be to give one coin to both pirate 1 and pirate 3, and thus keep ninety-eight coins for himself.

Chapter VI

Review of Critical Business Concepts

INTRODUCTION TO BUSINESS CONCEPTS

Many of you reading this book have a business or management background, and will already be quite familiar with most of the business concepts that will be discussed in the following. Regardless of whether you have already seen or studied these frameworks, it is recommended that you review these concepts again, as they will prove helpful during your interviews.

During a business case, it is recommended that you start with the frameworks explained earlier on cracking business cases. However, the more you practice and become comfortable with these frameworks, the more you will start to notice that you can additionally integrate business concepts, when relevant, to improve and strengthen your business case analysis.

When integrating one or more business concepts into your analysis, you should never literally name the business concept you will be using, but rather explain its idea. You should, for example, never say, "...and in order to analyze the industry attractiveness, I will apply the Porter's five forces model." Instead, you could say: "...and in order to analyze the industry attractiveness, it seems a good idea to take a better look at the industry competitors, the substitutes, the potential new entrants, the suppliers, and the buyers." As you will see, most of these frameworks and concepts are often fairly simple to understand, and using them correctly to tackle a business case can greatly enhance your analysis.

In the following, you will find an overview of the most important business concepts. Overall, they are easy to understand, and you can integrate them quite easily where relevant within the frameworks used to crack business cases. Several of these concepts are demonstrated through the use of a practical interview example. For a more detailed discussion of these concepts, as well as additional business concepts, please refer to academic and professional business literature.

OVERVIEW OF THE MOST IMPORTANT BUSINESS CONCEPTS AND IDEAS

Best-practice benchmarking

Best-practice benchmarking is a technique that will often be part of a business cases. It is the process of comparing a company's business efficiency and performance metrics relative to the industry's top performers. These top-performing companies are referred to as the best-practice firms, and are often the subject of studies aimed at better understanding what drives their success. Realizing a benchmarking study can lead to valuable insights on how to improve a company's performance. Notice that there are several types of benchmarking, such as process benchmarking, financial benchmarking, product benchmarking, and so on.

Successful benchmarking consists of first identifying some of your key problem areas for improvement. The next step is to identify similar organizations that use the same type of processes, as well as the firms that are leaders in these areas. Then you need to obtain information, generally through neutral organizations or mutual exchange of data, to better understand how these companies achieve this high performance. The last step is then to implement new business practices based on the findings of the benchmarking process.

An interview example:

Interviewer: […] so how would you evaluate whether our client's supply chain is efficient or not?

You: Well, we could do a benchmarking analysis, by investigating some key efficiency parameters of our client's supply chain, and compare these with the best practice companies with similar supply chains in the industry.

Interviewer: That is a good idea. Let us say that we found out that some of the best-practice companies have the following values for these key efficiency parameters […]

Capital Asset Pricing Model (CAPM)

The Capital Asset Pricing Model, also referred to as CAPM, is a methodology to determine a theoretically reasonable rate of return of an asset, and is often used in financial business cases. The CAPM is often used to determine a rate of return for the net present value formula, which will be detailed later on. The CAPM is also used to assess whether a given rate of return of a certain asset in a portfolio is reasonable or not, taking into account the asset's risk. The CAPM is calculated using the following formula:

Equation 1

$$E(R_i) = R_f + \beta_i(E(R_m) - R_f),$$

where $E(R_i)$ is the expected return of the asset i, R_f is the risk-free interest rate (for instance the interest rate on most government bonds), β_i is the relation between the asset i's return and the market return, and $E(R_m)$ is the expected return of the market.

The CAPM states that the expected return of an asset or stock is determined by two variables. On one hand, the time value of money (represented by R_f), and on the other hand, the risk of the stock itself (represented by β_i). The more volatile the returns of the asset are relative to the market average, the higher the β_i value will be (notice that the market itself has a Beta of 1.0 by definition). Approximate values for R_f, β_i, and $E(R_m)$ can be found online; however, in business cases, it is generally more important to demonstrate your understanding of the logic behind the formula than to make an accurate estimation of the expected return of the asset. Having some basic insights about historical returns is however advised in order to make sure that your assumptions are realistic.

An interview example:

Interviewer: […] another option our client is considering is investing some of its saved capital in a mid-sized biotechnology company. Our client requires an average expected annual return higher than 6 percent given the risk of the investment; do you think this is reasonable?

You: Would the investment in the biotechnology firm solely be seen as a stock investment, or should it rather be seen as a strategic acquisition?

Interviewer: It would purely be a stock investment. Why?

You: Well, in case the investment would be a strategic acquisition, then there might be additional important advantages besides the expected return of the asset, such as for example synergies. We could use the capital asset pricing model to see whether an expected annual return of 6 percent is reasonable. First of all, a good approximation for the risk-free interest rate would be the long-term US Treasury bill interest rate, which averages about 3.5 percent. A good approximation for $E(R_m)$ would be the S&P 500's adjusted long-term annual growth rate, which would be about 8.5 percent. The approximation for β_1 might be a little bit harder. Given that the asset in this case is a biotech firm, returns are probably more volatile relative to the overall market. Furthermore, the company is probably not yet an established biotech firm, as it is a mid-sized firm. Therefore, we could assume a β_1 of, let us say, 1.2. Bringing all this together, we find an expected return for the asset of 3.5 percent + 1.2 × (8.5 percent – 3.5 percent) = 9.5 percent. We thus find, using the CAPM, a required annual rate of return for the biotechnology stock of 9.5 percent.

Interviewer: What does this mean?

You: Well, our client requires an average expected annual return higher than 6 percent, but given the risk of this investment, represented by β_1, an average expected return of 9.5 percent annually should be required.

Interviewer: That seems about right.

Core competencies

Core competencies are those capabilities that are critical to a company to achieve a competitive advantage. Examples of a competitive advantage are cost-leadership, strong differentiation, or expert staff. Given the complexity of a business, management should always focus a considerable amount of its efforts on those competencies that really affect competitive advantage. Eventually these core competencies are the key areas of expertise, and are distinctive to the firm and critical to the long-term sustainability and growth.

Cost-benefit analysis

A cost-benefits analysis is a simple tool that can help structure your thinking and is often used to make final recommendations. The idea behind the cost-benefit analysis is to weigh the pros and the cons of a problem in order to make a decision. The more accurate you are in determining the merits and the drawbacks, the more accurate your analysis will be. Notice that the Net Present Value, which is explained further on, is a form of cost-benefit analysis where you quantitatively weigh the revenue streams against the cost and investment streams.

Economies of scale and economies of scope

Economies of scale refer to the decrease in the cost per unit as the production output increases. Economies of scope, on the other hand, is the theory that the average cost of goods decreases as a result of changes in the scope of for instance marketing, distribution, the number of different products manufactured, and so on. Economies of scale and scope however do not last, and at some point, the efficiencies start to become less effective (often referred to as diseconomies of scale or scope).

Net Present Value (NPV)

The Net Present Value (NPV) is a very important concept in the finance world, and can be very helpful in business cases where you have to assess investments. The concept is based on the fact that one dollar today is worth more than one dollar in the future. Therefore, in order to compare investments and their respective returns over time, you will first need to "discount" the value to its present value. The rate used to discount, also referred to as the discount rate, is driven by the speed of which money loses its value.

The NPV formula can be defined as:

Equation 2

$$NPV = \sum_{t=1}^{n} \frac{C_t}{(1+r)^t} - C_0,$$

where C_t is the investment's return in year t, C_0 is the initial investment in year 0, and r is the discount rate (in percent).

The general rule is that when the NPV is negative, one should not pursue the investment opportunity. On the other hand, a positive NPV implies that the investment opportunity is attractive.

A simple mathematical example:

A company has the opportunity to invest $1M euro today and would then obtain a return of $575K euro after one year and $650K euro after two years. The project is quite risky and has a relatively high discount rate of 15 percent. Should they make this investment?

Equation 3

$$\text{NPV} = \frac{(575K)}{(1+0.15)^1} + \frac{(650K)}{(1+0.15)^2} - 1M = -8.5K$$

Since the NPV is negative, the company should theoretically not pursue the investment opportunity.

An interview example:

Interviewer: […] and therefore, the organization is thinking about investing in a new production plant. How would you go about analyzing whether this is a good idea?

You: Well, we could look at the total investment cost (C_0), and estimate the revenue streams (C_t) we would be having over the following years. When we then estimate a reasonable discount rate (r), we have enough information to calculate the net present value. If the NPV is positive, it would be worth making the investment. If on the other hand the NPV would be negative, the company should likely not pursue this opportunity.

Interviewer: That seems like a good approach to start with.

Network effects

A network effect is the effect that one additional user of a certain product or service has on the value of that product or service to the other users. A classic example is a fax machine; if only one person would have a fax machine, it would be quite useless. When, however, more people start buying one, the value of a fax machine increases for those who already possess one. Network effects will often be useful in IT related business cases.

Porter's five forces

Porter's five forces is one of the most well-known frameworks used in business schools, and was developed by Harvard Business School professor Michael Porter. The framework is commonly used for industry analysis and business strategy development. The objective is to determine an industry's attractiveness or a firm's current strategic position. This is realized by investigating the competitive intensity within that industry and its market. More precisely, the analysis is realized by investigating a firm's direct industry competitors, the threat of new entrants in this industry, the threat of substitutes and the power of the firm's suppliers and buyers. An attractive industry would be one where the overall industry profitability is high, given the five forces, and an unattractive industry one where the overall industry profitability would be low.

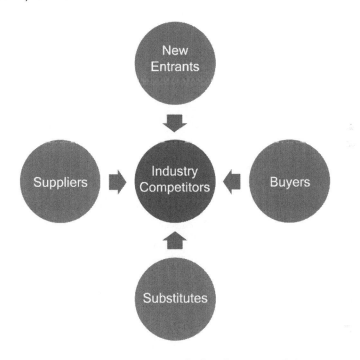

Exhibit 15 - The Porter's five forces model

Consultants often use this framework as a starting point to evaluate a client's position within its industry. Notice that for firms that are present in various industries, an analysis should be completed for each industry separately. The following provides an overview of the most important things you would need to investigate for each of the five forces:

- **Industry competitors:** Competitive strategy, pricing, and total advertising spending
- **New entrants:** Entry barriers, sunk costs, brand equity, and government policies
- **Substitutes:** Product differentiation, switching costs, and relative price

- **Suppliers:** Supplier competition and substitute inputs
- **Buyers:** Sales volume, price sensitivity and substitute products

An interview example:

Interviewer: [...] and the management is therefore wondering whether it should start selling high-end computer joysticks. How would you analyze whether this is a good opportunity to pursue or not?

You: We could start by first analyzing the industry attractiveness of the high-end computer joystick market by assessing the current competitors in this industry, the potential new entrants, the possible substitutes, as well as the suppliers and buyers in the industry. In case the market appears attractive, we could next analyze our client's core capabilities to see whether it would be a feasible move for our client and how they should approach this new market.

Interviewer: That seems like a good approach. Could you make a quick analysis of the industry attractiveness?

You: Well, let us start with the potential competition. In case our client would enter the market, would it have many industry competitors?

Interviewer: Currently one leading company dominates the market of the more economical models, and there are some smaller players focusing on the high-end models.

You: Given that our client wants to focus on the high-end market, this would mean that our client would compete against small players, which is generally easier than competing against a company that dominates the market. Let us now have a look at the potential substitutes. I would imagine that a computer mouse and a keyboard could be substitutes for a joystick, but they would never be perfect substitutes given that it cannot provide the exact same experience to the gamer. This is definitely valid for the more high-end joysticks [...]

Portfolio theory

The portfolio theory is an investment theory, which attempts to maximize the expected return for a given amount of portfolio risk or to minimize the portfolio risk for a given expected return on the portfolio by carefully choosing the proportions of the various assets in the portfolio.

These portfolio assets could be shares or bonds, but could, in another context, also be a set of daughter companies owned by the parent company. Portfolio theory often comes back in financial business cases, but it can also be relevant in strategy-related business cases.

Product life cycle

The product life cycle concept can be very helpful in business cases where you have to analyze a company's product or portfolio of products, and it is an interesting addition to the 4P's framework (marketing mix) which will be discussed further on. Often in business cases, part of the reason why sales are declining or costs are too high relative to revenues, can be found in the product's life cycle.

The idea is that every product has a "life span"; after it is launched, it grows and reaches a maximum number of sales, after which sales start to decline. Clearly, during each product life cycle, the appropriate product strategy is different and should be adjusted as the product moves through the succession of stages. When a product for instance is just introduced in the market, the costs of launching it are fairly high, whereas sales are generally low. Over time, through successful management, sales start to increase, production costs go down through economies of scale, and profitability increases. At some point however, the market demand decreases and profitability becomes more of a challenge.

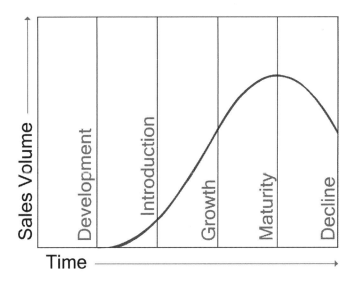

Exhibit 16 - The product life cycle concept

The 2×2-matrix

The 2×2-matrix is a business tool that is often very helpful during business cases. The idea is to visualize information more easily, by plotting one variable on a horizontal axis, and one variable on a vertical axis, creating four different quadrants. One very famous example of a 2×2-matrix is the BCG matrix, named after the Boston Consulting Group (BCG). This 2×2-matrix measures a company's relative market share on the horizontal axis and the market growth on the vertical axis.

An interview example:

Interviewer: One of our client's would like to invest a significant amount of his capital in the stock market. Which factors would you consider to be important when making such investments? Could you furthermore come up with a simple visualization to initially assess investment opportunities, taking into account that the client is quite risk-averse.

You: The two most important factors to consider when making investments are probably the rate of return of the investment, and the risk related to the investment. Given that our client is not willing to take too much risk, the client could use the following simple decision-making model to initially assess his investment opportunities:

Return on Investment (ROI)	High	Realize a detailed due diligence	Buy!
	Low	Don't buy!	Realize a quick due diligence
		High	Low
		Investment risk	

Exhibit 17 - An example of a 2×2-matrix for investment opportunities

Interviewer: That seems like a good visualization, [...]

The 7s framework

The 7s framework is definitely a McKinsey & Company favorite, and has been developed as a tool for investigating organizational effectiveness. This business concept is for example used to investigate a company's performance, or to align departments and processes for instance during a merger or a restructuring.

The idea is that all the elements of the framework — strategy, structure, systems, shared values, skills, style, and staff — need to be aligned in order for an organization to be effective and to sustain a competitive advantage. In case something in the organization is not working well, chances are that there are inconsistencies between some of the elements of the 7s framework. Once these inconsistencies are revealed, you can work to align the elements to make sure that they are all contributing to the shared goals and values of the organization.

Hard Elements	Soft Elements
• Strategy	• Shared Values
• Structure	• Skills
• Systems	• Style
	• Staff

Exhibit 18 - The 7s framework

Notice that the "hard elements" in the framework are generally influenced by the management, whereas the "soft elements" are less tangible and more driven by the organizational culture.

The marketing mix

The marketing mix, also referred to as the 4 P's, can come in very helpful during business cases. This business concept is often helpful in marketing or sales related business cases. The idea is to analyze a company's products/services, sales locations, prices and promotions relative to its competitors, along a set of standard questions. The following lists the most common questions per element of the framework, but you should always add your own questions.

- **Product:** Have the products/services and/or their packaging changed recently (at our company or at the competition)?
- **Place:** Have the sales channels changed, or are there new sales channels (at our company or at the competition)?
- **Price:** Did prices change recently (at our company or at the competition)?
- **Promotion:** Have there recently been (un)successful marketing campaigns (at our company or at the competition)?

The marketing mix framework is often incorporated in the product-pillar of the business situation framework, and is generally simply visualized as follows:

Exhibit 19 - The marketing mix concept

An interview example:

Interviewer: [...] and the sales of cookies have risen significantly recently, but the CEO is not really sure why! Could you investigate what has happened?

You: Well, we could have a look at the price of the cookies, the locations where they are sold, the recent promotions and eventually the product itself.

Interviewer: That seems like a good approach!

You: Did the company recently lower the price of its cookies? Or did the competition maybe increase its prices?

Interviewer: No, prices remained unchanged.

You: How about the sales channels? Did the company set up new sales channels, or did the sales channels that were already present started selling more efficiently?

Interviewer: No new sales channels were created, and the current sales channels did not become more efficient.

You: Was there maybe a recent promotion that was particularly success-ful? Or was there a recent publication benefiting to the sales of cookies? Or maybe even a marketing blunder of a key competitor?

Interviewer: No, these things did not occur.

You: Well, maybe something changed about the product? Did the com-pany recently change the ingredients of the cookies, or maybe the pack-aging of the product has changed?

Interviewer: The packaging of the product did not change. But the com-pany indeed made a change in the product recipe, making the cookies significantly crispier.

You: Did the company's competitors also do this? And was this decision to change the product recipe based upon a marketing study?

Interviewer: The competitors have so far stayed with the old recipe. But, a recent marketing study indicated that crispier cookies are getting more in demand.

You: Well, it seems to me that the increase in cookie sales is mainly due to the change in the product recipe.

Interviewer: That indeed seems like a good explanation.

Along with the 4 P's, there is a similar framework known as the 4 C's. This framework also analyses along four dimensions, and is also used in marketing cases. The idea is to analyze the consumer needs, the cost of the product or service, the convenience to buy it, and the communication in the media. This approach is more customer-oriented than the 4 P's approach, and is often used in business cases in which you need to better understand the customers and their needs.

SWOT analysis

SWOT analysis is a well-known framework used to evaluate a project or a business venture, but is, however, less commonly used in business cases. The analysis is popular with managers to help them with the strategic planning, for instance by identifying potential areas for improvement or determining the feasibility of a project or venture.

The idea of the SWOT analysis is to evaluate the internal and exter-nal factors that are favorable and unfavorable, relative to an initially de-termined business objective. This is realized through a careful analysis of a project's or a business venture's strengths and weaknesses (internal factors), as well as its opportunities and threats (external factors). The SWOT analysis is often simply visualized as follows.

Exhibit 20 - The SWOT analysis concept

An interview example:

Interviewer: [...] and, therefore, the CEO of FrostCo, a frozen foods company operating in France, would like to know whether his company is ready to start selling its products in the Spanish market.

You: We could quickly have a look at the company's strengths and weaknesses, as well as the opportunities and threats relative to this objective.

Interviewer: That seems like a good idea to start with.

You: Let us first have a look at the internal factors, namely the strengths and weaknesses of FrostCo. Given its strong cash position, it has enough capital to fund an entry into the Spanish market. On the other hand, the company has no experience selling its products outside of France, which will be a challenge since the Spanish frozen foods market is quite different. When we now consider the external factors, we could say that the Spanish market forms a great opportunity as it has so far been underserved in frozen foods. On the other hand, a significant threat might come from the several other frozen foods companies that are starting their operations in Spain. Overall, it can thus be said that the Spanish market forms a great opportunity, and the resources to enter the market seem to be available. On the other hand, FrostCo will first need to better understand the Spanish market, and analyze into detail the competitive landscape.

Interviewer: Let us do that. How would you then investigate the Spanish market? […]

ADDITIONAL READINGS ON BUSINESS CONCEPTS

Keep in mind that the previous overview is only a small summary of some of the most important business concepts. Understanding these, and being able to apply them, will most definitely help you to better solve business cases. Nonetheless, there are several other business concepts that could be helpful during a business case, as this list is definitely not exhaustive. For this reason, it is advised that you in addition study other business concepts from qualitative academic and professional literature.

Appendix A

Overview of Consulting Buzzwords

As in any industry, the consulting industry uses several buzzwords. It is important to be aware of these specific terms when going on a consulting interview. Therefore, in the following, an overview of the most common buzzwords used by consultants has been included.

The 80/20 rule: The idea that you can get 80 percent of the answer in 20 percent of the time. The other 80 percent of your time might not be worth it, as 80 percent of the answer is often already sufficient to decide on further actions.

Adjacencies: Refers to markets or businesses that are not too far away from a companies' core business in terms of technology, sales channels, brand etc.

At the end of the day: A phrase used by consultants to summarize a discussion, and perhaps to close off certain avenues of discussion.

BCG matrix: The BCG matrix, also referred to as the growth/share matrix, is a portfolio assessment tool developed by the Boston Consulting Group. The matrix shows the market growth rate versus relative market share and is often used to optimize the corporate portfolio, achieve effective resource allocation, or better understand the marketplace.

Benchmarking: The process of comparing one's business processes and performance metrics against those of other companies (often the best performing companies) in the industry.

Big 3: McKinsey, Bain and BCG (also referred to as MBB).

Big 4: Deloitte, Ernst & Young, KPMG, and PricewaterhouseCoopers.

Blank slide: An initial sketch on paper, made before the actual analysis, to show what the slide should look like eventually in the case presentation (called blank because it does not yet include the data that the analysts will input).

Boiling the ocean: Refers to an impossible task; by making things so complex that you could never achieve your goals. Generally, when a project manager or partner says, "Let's not boil the ocean," it means the team should not be overly concerned with all the small details.

Bottom-up analysis: Method that starts by looking at the smallest units possible to initiate an analysis, and then gradually works its way up by looking at the larger blocks (contrary to top-down analysis).

Buckets: Often used as a synonym for categories.

Business Process Re-engineering (BPR): The process of rethinking (and usually downsizing) a client's business processes by eliminating unneeded or "non-value-adding" tasks and then implementing more efficient ones.

Buy-in: Often used as a synonym for reaching agreement or support.

CAGR: The Compound Annual Growth Rate, which is the year-on-year growth rate of an investment over a specified period of time.

Case team: The team working on a consulting project for a client; traditionally composed of one partner, one manager, one consultant, and two or more analysts.

Core client: Refers to a client with which the consulting firm has a long-standing relationship, and one with which there is generally continuous communication even if there are no ongoing projects.

Core competencies: The areas in which a company excels, and that enable a business to deliver unique value to its customers. The general belief is that a company should only enter those businesses that relate to their core competencies.

Crunching numbers: Refers to making a large amount of calculations on a data set. For associate consultants this often implies literally hours of work in MS Excel. Often the term "being crunched" is also used to refer to consultants that are having an extremely high workload.

DCF: The Discounted Cash Flow, which is the present value of future cash flows.

Deck: A report, generally in the form of PowerPoint slides, discussing the client issues and the recommendations from the project team. A consultant that is "writing the deck" is preparing the slides/report for presentation to the client.

Deliverable: An output produced by the case team, as a result of the project that is intended to be delivered to the client.

Due diligence: Refers to an investigation of a business, prior to signing a contract.

EBIT: Earnings before Interest and Taxes

EBITDA: Earnings before Interest, Taxes, Depreciation, and Amortization.

Elevator test: A test to assess one's ability to summarize in a short time (typically thirty seconds). The elevator test represents the hypothetical situation in which you are sharing the elevator with a CEO, and need to give him or her a quick overview of the results of the analysis during the ride.

Engagement: A consulting assignment; also referred to as a case or a project.

Experience curve: The principle that a company's cost declines as its production increases. An experience curve that depicts a 20 percent cost reduction for every doubling in total production is called an "80 percent experience curve." Most experience curves among different industries range from 75 to 90 percent.

Granular: Refers to the basic elements that make up a business problem; often used in the context of increasing the fineness/granularity of an analysis.

High-level: Also referred to as a "50,000-foot or a 5,000-mile view," which refers to a very basic analysis to provide an overview of a situation without going into the details.

Hurdle rate: The minimum return rate a company is willing to accept on a project. Generally, if the return on an investment exceeds the hurdle rate, the company should make the investment.

Implementation: The practical realization of the advice a consulting firm gave to its client.

Key: Synonym for critical, essential or important.

Learning curve: The rate at which someone acquires knowledge. A consultant, for instance, needs to be able to acquire as quickly as possible background information or industry knowledge at the start of a new case. A steep learning curve is clearly a good thing.

Letter of Proposal: A sales document proposed to a potential client that describes how and on what a consulting team would focus its efforts to improve the client's business.

Leverage: A synonym for *use*, as in "The firm should leverage its most important resources."

Low-hanging fruits: Synonym for quick wins. For instance, simple and quick analyses that are easiest to cover and can provide some first insights.

MECE: Mutually Exclusive, Collectively Exhaustive. When data have to be MECE, it means that the data in a group should be divided into subgroups that comprehensively represent that group, without any overlapping.

NPV: Net Present Value, which is the sum of a series of discounted cash flows. The NPV is often used to assess the profitability of an investment or a project.

O'Hare test: A test used by interviewers to assess whether your personality would fit the corporate culture. They basically ask themselves the following question, "If I were stuck overnight with this person at O'Hare Airport, would I have fun?"

On the beach: Refers to being between two case assignments. When consultants are "on the beach," their weekly working hours usually drop significantly. Generally, when consultants are on the beach, they usually study management books, arrange their computer files, or help making proposals.

Opportunity cost: A key concept in economics, referring to the cost of the next best alternative available among the choices you chose from.

Outsourcing: Hiring an external provider to perform a task traditionally performed within a company, usually realized at a lower cost. Examples of services that are commonly outsourced are call center services and accounting services.

Progress review: A periodic meeting, either internal or with the client, to discuss the progress that has been made over the preceding period.

ROS/RMS graph: A graph, which shows the profitability (usually thus the ROS) versus the relative market share for a certain industry.

Rightsizing: Also known as "downsizing." This is a term used for restructuring a company. It is generally used to refer to headcount reductions, but it can also be used for other types of restructuring, such as production plant, office, technology, or process restructurings.

Scope: Refers to the set of deliverables that has been agreed upon at the beginning of a client engagement.

Shareholder value: Refers to the total wealth a company generates for all its shareholders combined. The primary objective of a case team during most engagements is to maximize the shareholder value.

Skill set: Consultants often use this term to refer to the skills needed to be a successful consultant. The most important skills in the consultant skill set are generally analytical and reasoning skills, as well as interpersonal skills.

Stakeholder: A person or organization that has a stake in the outcome of a particular action. Most often the stakeholders in a case would be the shareholders, employees, customers or creditors.

Supply chain: The entire system involved in physically distributing a product or service from the supplier to the customer.

Takeaway: Refers to the most important point that should be remembered upon the conclusion of a discussion.

Taking the lead: A phrase often used by more experienced consultants when they wish to pass on a task to a less experienced consultant. When this phrase is used, it usually refers to a tedious task that does not require any leadership skills.

Thinking outside of the box: Refers to thinking creatively or from a new perspective. When someone says, "Let's think outside of the box," that person usually means that he or she is looking for new ideas.

Transparency: An indication for openness. When a consultant says, "We will be transparent," then the person is implying that he or she will be particularly revelatory on certain issues. Often, it also implies that the consultant has been rather opaque up to then.

Top-down analysis: Method that starts by looking at the bigger picture (usually high-level) to initiate an analysis, and then gradually works its way down (also referred to as "drilling down") by looking at the individual blocks that make the bigger picture (contrary of bottom-up analysis).

Up or out: An employee promotion policy that is used by several consulting firms, and implies that if you are not promoted (up), you will have to leave (out) the firm.

Upward feedback: The process of providing feedback by junior employees "upward" to the more senior employees, such as managers and partners.

Value-added: The amount by which the value of goods or services are increased by each stage in the value chain. Companies try to maximize the value addition over the entire value chain, as this improves their competitive position. Value-added can also refer to the extra features given to a product/service that go beyond standard expectations, often without significant cost increases.

Venture capital (VC): The equity-related financial capital provided to high-potential start-ups in their early stage. Before providing venture capital, the venture capital funds will usually carry out a detailed due diligence. To increase the likelihood of success of the start-up, venture capitalists generally also look after the companies in which they invest.

WAG: Stands for wild-ass guess, and is an estimate based upon professional experience. WAGs are often used when there is no time to do all the necessary research to come up with a good approximation, in which case a consultant would use his experience based upon previous cases to make the estimation/guess.

White space opportunity: An opportunity for a company to make money in a business area in which it is currently not present. Often refers to adjacencies, outside of the company's traditional business boundaries.

Work plan: Also referred to as a "project plan" and is the schedule used to complete a consulting engagement. It specifies how the project will be conducted and sets the deadlines and responsibilities.

Appendix B

Basic Overview of the Financial Report

Whether you have a financial background or not, most consulting firms will expect you to have at least a basic understanding of financial statements. Since these are well structured and easy to understand, you can easily get an adequate understanding. Most larger firms have the obligation to make their financial statements public, and they can often be found on their corporate website. It is recommended that you first have a look at some examples to get comfortable with the format. In general, the report consists of four financial statements that describe the financial health of a company:

- The balance sheet
- The income statement
- The statement of retained earnings
- The statement of cash flows

Often additional notes supplement a company's annual report, to describe certain items in the financial report in further detail. In general smaller firms use simplified versions of the financial statements, and larger firms have a more complex financial report. The next four sections will briefly cover each of the four financial statements. Notice that all values between parentheses in the examples represent negative values.

THE BALANCE SHEET

The balance sheet provides an overview of a company's assets, liabilities, and equity at one specific point in time. It is often referred to as a "snapshot" of what a firm looks like on a certain moment. When analysts perform a financial analysis of a firm, they base most of their financial ratios on the balance sheet.

On the left side of the balance sheet, you can find the assets, which represent the economic resources of a company. They are listed in order of how easily they can be converted to cash. A company always obtains these assets by incurring debt (liabilities), or by obtaining new investors and using retained earnings (equity). The liabilities and equity can be found on the right side of the balance sheet, and are listed in order of when they become due for payment. Given the relationship between on the one side assets and on the other side liabilities and equity, both sides of the balance sheet always have to be equal to each other. Exhibit 21 is a basic example of a balance sheet.

Balance Sheet MediaCo
31 December, 2010 ($ in thousands)

ASSETS

Cash	$2,000
Bank accounts	$5,000
Accounts receivable	$1,000
Inventory	$3,000
Equipment	$6,000
Buildings & land	$14,000
Total assets:	$31,000

LIABILTIES

Current liabilities	$3,000
Taxes payable	$1,000
Long-term liabilities	$10,000

EQUITY

Capital stock	$15,000
Retained earnings	$2,000
Total liabilities & equity	$31,000

Exhibit 21 - Example of a balance sheet

THE INCOME STATEMENT

The income statement, or profit and loss statement (P&L), presents the results of a firm's business operations over a period of time. It explains how revenue has been transformed into net income after all the expenses have been deducted. The net income is often also informally referred to as the "bottom line." Exhibit 22 is an example of an income statement.

Income Statement MediaCo
Year Ending 31/12/2010 ($ in thousands)

Revenue	$ 7,000
– Cost of goods sold (COGS)	$(3,000)
= Gross profit	**$4,000**
– Sales, Gen. & Admin. expenses (SG&A)	$(1,000)
= Operating margin (EBIT)	**$3,000**
(+/–) interest income/expenses	$(500)
= Earnings before tax (EBT)	**$2,500**
– Tax expenses	$(500)
= Net income	**$2,000**

Exhibit 22 - Example of an income statement

THE STATEMENT OF RETAINED EARNINGS

The statement of retained earnings provides an overview of what the management is doing with the earnings of a company. In general, the management can choose between investing the earnings back in the business or distributing them to the shareholders. The retained earnings are generally calculated as follows: Ending Retained Earnings = Beginning Retained Earnings - Dividends Paid + Net Income. Exhibit 23 is an example of a statement of retained earnings.

Statement of Retained Earnings MediaCo
01/01/2010 - 12/31/2010 ($ in thousands)

Retained earnings (begin of 2010)	$ 2,000
Net income	$ 2,000
Dividends paid	$(2,000)
Retained earnings (end of 2010)	**$ 2,000**

Exhibit 23 - Example of a statement of retained earnings

THE STATEMENT OF CASH FLOWS

The statement of cash flows essentially shows the flow of cash in and out of the business, and gives you an idea about a firm's liquidity and solvency. It is often considered the most important statement, as it shows whether a company is holding or generating sufficient cash to sustain its business activities. The cash flows are broken down into three different sources of cash generation, namely, operating, investing, and financing cash flows. Exhibit 24 is a simplified example of a statement of cash flows.

Simplified Statement of Cash Flows, MediaCo
01/01/2010 - 12/31/2010 ($ in thousands)

Cash flows from operations	$ 11,000
Cash flows from investing	$(3,000)
Cash flows from financing	$(1,000)
Net cash flow	**$7,000**

Exhibit 24 - Example of a statement of cash flows

Appendix C

Review of Other Sources on Cracking Consulting Interviews

The objective of this book is to provide you with the most important information needed to succeed in your case interviews. When you have studied this book, and internalized its concepts and frameworks, you should have built up a strong set of case interview skills. Nonetheless, extra readings and studying other materials could help you to further increase your chances of success. For this reason, an overview of several additional sources on case interviews, both commercial and non-commercial, has been included. Please note that the authors of these sources are in no way related to this book, and the use of these sources is completely up to the reader.

Recommended freely available resources:

- All the websites of the leading consulting firms
- www.aceyourcase.com (free newsletter & articles)
- www.caseinterview.com (free newsletter & video tutorials)

Recommended commercially available resources:

- "Look Over My Shoulder Program" by V. Cheng
- "Guesstimation: Solving the World's Problems on the Back of a Cocktail Napkin" by L. Weinstein

- "The Boston Consulting Group on Strategy: Classic Concepts and New Perspectives" by Carl W. Stern and M. S. Deimler
- "The Pyramid Principle: Logic in Writing and Thinking" by B. Minto
- "What I Didn't Learn in Business School: How Strategy Works in the Real World "by J. Barney and P. G. Clifford
- "Profit from the Core: A Return to Growth in Turbulent Times" by C. Zook and J. Allen
- "The McKinsey Engagement: A Powerful Toolkit For More Efficient and Effective Team Problem Solving" by P. N. Friga
- Any business strategy related article published in 'The Economist' or 'Harvard Business Review'

About the Author

Tom Rochtus was born and raised in Belgium. He has a bachelor's degree in management from the University of Leuven in addition to a master's degree in management of technology from the Louvain School of Management, where he graduated magna cum laude. He has furthermore spent several years traveling and studying abroad; including a master's degree in International Business at Egade in Monterrey (Mexico), and an academic exchange at the University of Edinburgh (U.K). His professional career started when early at university, he set up his own successful information technology company, and participated in and won awards at prominent competitions for innovative young entrepreneurs. As part of his master's degree, he completed an internship at Procter & Gamble as a strategy planner, which eventually inspired him to pursue a career in management consulting. After successfully applying for the leading management consulting firms, Tom eventually signed with Bain & Company, one of the world's most prestigious management consulting companies. During his free time, he enjoys traveling to "offbeat" destinations, as well as spending time with his family and friends.

Acknowledgments

Thanks to everyone who had a hand in making this book possible. Definitively to CreateSpace Inc. and to Amazon Inc. for all their help in the editorial, production and distribution processes. Furthermore a special thanks to Ana Llerenas for designing all the images and the cover of this book, but mostly for her continuous support throughout the whole process. To end, I would also like to thank all my friends and family, especially my father, for being a constant source of joy and support in everything I do. Thank you!

Printed in Great Britain
by Amazon